Logical Positivism Revisited

Logical Positivism Revisited

Kunchapudi Srinivas

D.K. Printworld (P) Ltd.
Publishers of Indian Traditions

Cataloging in Publication Data — DK
[Courtesy: D.K. Agencies (P) Ltd. <docinfo@dkagencies.com>]

Srinivas, K. (Kunchapudi), 1955-
Logical positivism revisited / Kunchapudi Srinivas.

p. cm.

Includes bibliographical references (p.) and index.

ISBN 13: 9788124605707
ISBN 10: 812460570X

1. Logical positivism. I. Title.

DDC 146.42 22

First published in India, 2011
ISBN 13: 978-81-246-0570-7 (HB) ISBN 10: 81-246-0570-X

Published and printed by:
D.K. Printworld (P) Ltd.
Regd. office : *'Srikunj,'* F-52, Bali Nagar
Ramesh Nagar Metro Station
New Delhi – 110 015
Phones : (011) 2545 3975; 2546 6019; *Fax* : (011) 2546 5926
E-mail: indology@dkprintworld.com
Web: www.dkprintworld.com

DEDICATED TO

My esteemed Teacher
(Late) Professor Suman Gupta

Preface

THE book *Logical Positivism Revisited* aims at examining the fundamental doctrines of logical positivism concerning ontology, epistemology and ethics. In the process, it introduces the reader to the basic tenets of classical empiricism of Locke, Berkeley, and Hume. As it is widely acknowledged, even by the logical positivists, logical positivism is an offshoot of Humean empiricism in a different linguistic garb. In spite of the fact that there is an apparent unanimity in the claim of logical positivists as regards the function of philosophy as "logical analysis of language," it appears that they seldom had unanimity on a number of key philosophical issues. However, these independent views did not really go against the very spirit of logical positivism in general. The present work, by and large, heavily relies on A.J. Ayer's account of logical positivism as expounded in his works. Ayer, as one understands him from his writings, is a prolific and thought-provoking writer. Not only that, Ayer is instrumental in disseminating the philosophy of logical positivism to the English-speaking world. His arguments are imbued with great profundity and lucidity. After the demise of the great analysts like Moore, Russell and Wittgenstein, although Wittgenstein was not a member of the Vienna Circle, the credit goes to Ayer who took over the reins of logical positivist movement in Britain and defended its fundamental doctrines until his death in 1989. Logical positivism as a movement revolutionised the entire philosophical circles in the West between the two world wars with its radical approach towards the problems of philosophy.

But it gradually lost its grip in the philosophical circles over a period of time. This is the case with every philosophical movement and logical positivism is not an exception to this rule. History of philosophy is a living testimony to this fact. The grand philosophical systems and movements of the past had to give way to the newer ones. There is always a noticeable shift in human thinking, living and feeling. This shift is attributed to the prevailing historical and socio-economic conditions which determine the limitations of the life-world in which we are placed. What is important to note here is that logical positivism provided us with a set of new tools and techniques of analysis. These new tools and techniques have completely transformed our old ways of thinking in the sense that there is more stress on clarity. What is ambiguous and opaque to our thought is completely dispensed with. We have to admit this fact. In a BBC interview with Bryan Maggie in 1971, Ayer admitted that "the future of pure linguistic philosophy is very bleak." This statement of Ayer clearly vindicates the openness of a thinker. But, contrary to Ayer's prediction, linguistic philosophy has been accorded due place in the writings of postmodern philosophers, and it continues to exert its influence in one form or another, for we cannot dispense with language at all.

Last but not least, I would like to express my deep and sincere gratitude to many of my friends who inspired me in bringing out this work. One of them is Dr Clement Lourdes, Associate Professor, Department of English, Pondicherry University, Puducherry. Certainly, I cannot forget the encouragement given by my other friends.

Oct., 2010 **K. Srinivas**
Puducherry

Contents

Introduction

EVERY age is said to be an age of transition. In the absence of transition there is no change in the life of human beings. But, transition is always viewed as a progressive revolt against the old ways of thinking, feeling, and living. Such a revolt becomes almost a natural necessity. The rapid developments in science and technology substantiate this view. Consequently, the modern developments in science and technology proved to be a serious threat not only to many existing scientific theories, but also to philosophical theories, concepts, and the various categories of experience. It is really a testing time for those schools of thought that claim to have affinity with science in some way or the other. As it is realised by the scientists and some philosophers of science, there is nothing like perfect or absolute knowledge. Knowledge is always relative. Within this relative knowledge we find an element of absoluteness. As a result of new developments in modern science, there is every need to reconstruct certain systems of philosophical thought which profess their adherence to scientific thinking. Logical positivism is one such school of thought which claims to have taste for science, mathematics and logic, and distaste for metaphysics of the transcendental kind.

A philosophical theory or a school of thought is called genuinely scientific in so far as it provides rational answers to the problems of philosophy. And the problems of philosophy are nothing but the problems of life. In other words, the importance of a philosophical theory or a school of thought lies in its interpretation of the various facets of human experience for better understanding. In order to face this challenge the major systems of philosophy or schools of thought have to keep pace with the modern developments in the field of science. As time passes the old theories of philosophy lose their significance and gradually become obsolete. Nevertheless, some of the basic tenets of the earliest systems of philosophy or schools of thought are assimilated into newer ones to show progress in the sphere of human knowledge. But there are philosophers who claim that philosophy being a reflective activity need not always take recourse to science in explaining the various facets of human experience, for science itself is found wanting in many respects. The brute reduction of human experiences to science and scientific form of investigation is an unwarranted blind belief in science. Such an attempt robs philosophy of its legitimate role in human life. The best way to resolve the stand-off between philosophy and science is to determine their respective roles in building up human knowledge. If science aims at the explanation of the world of facts, philosophy aims at the understanding of the nature of the world. The distinction between explanation and understanding brings out the distinctive nature of the methods followed by these two disciplines. Most of our scientific explanations are the outcome of the experimental method. Likewise, our understanding of any phenomenon is dependent on the reflective method. But logical positivists overlooked this distinction and attempted to explain the concepts of philosophy by borrowing the method of analysis from science. Their distaste for metaphysics prompted them to opt for the scientific method.

Now the question that arises is: What is the relation between science and philosophy? Many people are of the opinion that these disciplines are two poles apart. They believe that philosophy is an abstruse and the most abstract of all the disciplines, and it has nothing to do with mundane human experiences. Thus, they identify philosophy either with theology or metaphysics, especially with transcendental metaphysics. Partly, the philosophers of the ancient Greece and the medieval period are responsible for giving such a picture about philosophy. For instance, in Plato's philosophy, Plato erected an iron curtain between the phenomenal world (the world of becoming) and the world of Forms (the eternal world). Plato held that those who possess the knowledge of the world of Forms are really endowed with 'wisdom'. Thus in Plato's metaphysics the trans-empirical world, which is beyond human comprehension, is rated as higher order reality. The world of phenomena or the empirical world is only a carbon copy of the trans-empirical one. The medieval thinkers like St Augustine, St Thomas Aquinas, and St Anselm had God as central figure in their systems of thought. Even in the modern period, the philosophers like René Descartes, William Leibniz and George Berkeley clubbed theology with philosophy. However, the contributions of these philosophers to the history of ideas are not to be underrated or ignored. Every philosopher is directly or indirectly influenced by the existing historical and socio-economic conditions of the period in which he lived. A cursory look at the history of philosophy reveals this fact. The generations of philosophers have attempted to rectify the mistakes or errors committed by the earlier thinkers with a view to building a new philosophical system. Every new system is treated as a stepping stone for further progress in the field of human knowledge. These new developments in philosophy have changed the scope and the aim of philosophy considerably. This resulted in the denial speculative thinking in philosophy to make philosophy logically rigorous and scientific. Then the question before us is: What is philosophy? By all means, it is not all that easy to explain what philosophy is, for there are many interpretations. Each age in the history of philosophy interpreted philosophy in accordance with the requirements of that age. At one point of time philosophy was identified with theology, and at another point of time with metaphysics, and yet another point of time with epistemology, and so on. Therefore, it is very difficult to give a universally acceptable interpretation of philosophy. This does not mean that philosophy has no subject matter to deal with. At times, the students of philosophy are puzzled as they are not sure of the subject matter of philosophy. Philosophy as a reflective enterprise virtually covers everything under the sun. The problems of philosophy are basically the problems of life. For example, what is called 'science' now was known as natural philosophy at one point of time. But, after the renaissance, because of rapid industrialisation in the West, most of the specialised branches of the science gradually parted off from philosophy and sought independent existence. With the emergence of more human societies a number of new fields like economics, sociology, geography, anthropology, and linguistics have come into existence. As a result of these developments in modern times, the philosophers of analytic tradition felt that if we do not clearly define the subject matter of philosophy, then we have to concede that it belongs to a no man's land. To avoid this rather embarrassing situation they held that the subject matter of philosophy is language and its legitimate method is analysis. In other words, the function of philosophy is "logical analysis of language." But this is not true. One can at the most say this is one of the functions of philosophy, but not its sole function. In fact, to press our claim that philosophy accommodates almost all the disciplines, we can refer to various fields of study like philosophy of mathematics, philosophy of law, philosophy of social sciences, philosophy of environment, and so on.

Coming to the relation between science and philosophy, it is generally regarded that science is nothing but man's systematic and orderly knowledge of objective reality. Science aims at explanation of things or phenomena and is always persuasive. The basic postulates of science are rationality, observation, experimentation, prediction and hypothesis formation; whereas philosophy is concerned with the nature of reality and man's place in it. Philosophy aims at understanding the nature of various phenomena. A scientist is primarily concerned with empirical facts. But a philosopher is interested in interpreting these facts for making them more intelligible to humankind. A philosopher along with his powers of reason or intellect must also possess scientific temper to make the scope of philosophy more scientific and rational rather than speculative. In a way, both philosophy and science are complementary to each other, but not antithetical to each other.

Regarding the nature of the method, it is generally viewed that a method is a device or a procedure to obtain certain results in a specific field of research. In fact, there is a serious normative question concerning the method that should be employed in science. The development of science will not in itself establish the objectivity of the method employed, but the claim that a particular method is reasonable will be strengthened by showing that the method is typically the one employed in science. While ascribing or denying the validity to any method we can also examine the extent to which a method provides means of assessing hypotheses and theories in an impartial manner. It is believed that scientific inquiry unlike other methods of inquiry is objective by its very nature. The validity of any method lies in its power to explain things or phenomena in a coherent way. However, the important question before us is: Do all methods of inquiry advocated by various philosophers of science justify the objective nature of their approach? We have several methods of inquiry at our disposal. They are, for example, the inductive method of the positivists, the hypothetico-deductive method of Karl Popper, the retroductive method of Norwood Russell Hanson, the anarchist method of Paul Feyerabend and the paradigms of Thomas Kuhn, and so on. Each method claims its superiority over the other. They try to illustrate their superiority by taking a few examples from the history of science. It is true that each method had contributed to the development of science in some way or the other. At the same time, each method if studied in isolation from the other methods of inquiry is found to have some disadvantages. If one applies a particular method ignoring the role of other methods in the development of science, then one is certainly limiting the scope of human knowledge. In such a situation one should really look for a method which can accommodate all the basic postulates of science such as rationality, observation, experimentation, prediction and hypotheses formation. Such a method will have an overwhelming persuasive force. We use these postulates to unravel the secrets of Nature. Unfortunately, there is not even a single method which could accommodate all the basic postulates of science. The only possible way to have a genuine "scientific method" is to study the various methods of science in their interconnections to promote a "unified method of science." Perhaps, this might help us in comprehending the nature of science and the part played by the various methods of science in the development of scientific knowledge. Our sole objective in the course of this work would be to assess the supposedly scientific character of logical positivism as expounded by A.J. Ayer from the standpoint of the above-said "unified method of science."

Basically, the problems in epistemology arise out of the distinction between appearance and reality. Logical Positivism is one among those schools of thought, following the legacy of Hume, which abolish the distinction between appearance and reality. This school of thought is often referred to as "logical empiricism," or "scientific empiricism." In spite of its loud claim to stand for "logical and scientific foundations of human knowledge," this school of thought in particular is passing through a deep epistemological crisis because of an obvious and ever growing conflict between its theories and actual scientific proof. One of the principal programmes of logical positivists, also known as "Vienna Circle," is to eliminate "metaphysics" from the sphere of philosophy in order to make philosophy more logically rigorous and scientific than it used to be. According to logical positivists, those entities which transcend the limits of empirical verification or sensory experience fall under the category of "metaphysics." In other words, metaphysics is the doctrine that deals with super-sensible reality. Logical positivists are basically concerned with the metaphysics of the transcendental kind. There are other forms of metaphysics such as descriptive and revisionary ones. Strawson in his *Individuals* (1959) highlights these distinctions. He felt that there is nothing wrong on the part of an analytic philosopher if he indulges in descriptive metaphysics. The attempt of logical positivists to eliminate metaphysics of the transcendental kind from the sphere of philosophy is a genuine one. As a matter of fact, logical positivists started this programme (the elimination of metaphysics) with a good intention, but the question is whether they could really eliminate metaphysics from the sphere of philosophy. In the process of eliminating metaphysics from the sphere of philosophy, logical positivists committed a few mistakes. First of all, the principle of verification as a criterion to demarcate meaningful assertions from meaningless ones is vulnerable to serious criticism because it is formulated in such a way that it not only eliminates certain forms of metaphysical entities but also ethics and aesthetics from the purview of philosophical discussions. In fact, the attempt to eliminate metaphysics from the sphere of philosophy has both positive and negative features. The positive feature of such a campaign against metaphysics is that logical positivism is opposed to the traditional philosophical issues that are speculative, religious and idealistic in their nature and thereby showing little interest in the problems of scientific cognition. The negative aspect of such a campaign is that logical positivism has branded the issues like objectivity, necessity, causation and induction as metaphysical since they do not come under the purview of sense-experience. Consequently, they violated the fundamental tenets of empiricism. Logical positivists with their ontological and metaphysical framework cannot comprehend the real nature of these issues.

However, due recognition should be given to logical positivism as a school of thought for concentrating on a number of complex problems that occupied the minds of philosophers as well as scientists. Logical positivism can be credited with the development of logic of scientific cognition, and investigation into the specific problems of logic of science. There is no doubt that this school of thought attempted to get rid of speculative doctrines and dogmas from the philosophy to make philosophy a genuine branch of knowledge.

In this work I focused my attention on A.J. Ayer (1910-89), a leading British exponent of logical positivism. I have concentrated mainly on the ontological, epistemological and logical foundations of Ayer's logical positivism, and have made an attempt to examine it from the standpoint of science. Various problems of epistemology are discussed, not in isolation from one another, but in their interconnectedness. While discussing the basic issues of epistemology of logical positivism, I have attempted to deal with the issues that preoccupied logical positivists at different stages of evolution. At the same time I have emphasised the most general, fundamental problems connected with the nature of scientific knowledge, objective significance of scientific theories and the role of subject in the construction of scientific theories.

1

Classical British Empiricism and its Development

It is obvious that neither philosophy as world outlook (in its wider sense of the term) nor its history can be studied in fragments. The future philosophy of any sort must be based on the foundations of the past and present. Philosophical development in general is not a spontaneous activity, but is evolutionary. History of philosophy is nothing but history of ideas of the various thinkers and schools of thought belonging to different periods of time. By and large, such ideas are about nature of universe, ultimate constituents of reality, sources of knowledge, truth, nature of man, and man's place in Nature and society. The philosophical development of each thinker or school of thought, to a greater extent, is dependent upon the existing social conditions of his time. The flux in reality, natural as well as social, brings about certain changes in an individual's philosophical thinking. No single formulation or theory in philosophy or science or religion is immutable in this world of impermanence. Nevertheless, every formulation serves as a stepping stone for the development of future systems of thought.

Just as it is impossible to comprehend the philosophy of Aristotle without having a look at Plato's, the philosophy of logical positivism becomes incomprehensible without knowing the seminal doctrines of classical British empiricists (Locke, Berkeley and Hume). The influence of classical British empiricists, especially of Hume, is most striking on logical positivists. The philosophers of Vienna Circle are honest enough to accept that the cardinal principles of their doctrine (logical positivism) are taken from the classical British empiricism. A.J. Ayer, the leading exponent of logical positivism in England, while narrating the objectives of logical positivism in his most influential work *Language, Truth and Logic* writes:

> The views which are put forward in this treatise derive from the doctrines of Bertrand Russell and Wittgenstein, which are themselves the logical outcome of the empiricism of Berkeley and David Hume.[1]

Nevertheless, logical positivists claim that their empiricism differs from that of Hume because of its powerful "logical technique." To quote Ayer's remark in this context:

> Their (logical positivists') originality lay in their attempt to make it (empiricism) logically rigorous and in their use for the purpose of a developed and sophisticated logical technique.[2]

But for this professed novelty, namely, the introduction of a new "logical technique," logical positivism is a new wine in the same old bottle. It will be revealed in the course of this present work.

Empiricism as a theory of knowledge emerged in the early seventeenth century in Britain in opposition to continental rationalism. Rationalists, in general, hold the view that all genuine knowledge is possible through reason alone. Contrary to this view, empiricists hold that all knowledge originates in sense-experience alone. For both rationalists and empiricists ideas constitute knowledge. The fundamental difference

1. A.J. Ayer, *Language, Truth and Logic* (Harmondsworth, 1975), 2nd edn., p. 41.
2. A.J. Ayer, "The Vienna Circle", *The Revolution in Philosophy* (London, 1963), pp. 73-74.

between rationalism and empiricism lies in their treatment of justification of knowledge and source of ideas that constitute knowledge. René Descartes (1596-1650) declares that the indubitability of its (rationalism's) general principles provides the ground for accepting any theory. For empiricists, justification proceeds from observations to the most general principles of the theory. Then the acceptability or denial of any theory (proposition), for empiricists, rests on pure "observational data." This view of empiricists limits the role of human cognition, subsequently the scope of human knowledge.

Before discussing the basic tenets of empiricist theory of knowledge, it is necessary to state that theory of knowledge, which is supposed to be the science of cognition,[3] has two important dimensions, viz. (1) psychological, and (2) methodological. The psychological dimension of epistemology is said to be concerned with the cognitive acts such as the genesis of concepts, judgements, and thoughts in general. Then this problem belongs to psychology. In its methodological dimension, epistemology is said to be concerned with the cognitive results. In other words, it is concerned with the results of our cognitive processes and their relation to the objective reality. As a matter of fact, these two dimensions are inseparable from each other. It is not all that easy to make a watertight distinction between these two dimensions. However, being students of philosophy, we are concerned with the methodological aspects of empiricist theory of knowledge. With this end in view, we start with the epistemology of John Locke, who is supposed to be the pioneer of classical British empiricism.

JOHN LOCKE (1632-1704)

John Locke, a medical doctor by profession, wrote his famous

3. Ajdukiewicz, Kazimierz, *Problems and Theories of Philosophy*, tr. Henry Skolimowsky and Anthony Quinton (London, 1975), pp. 22-24.

work, *An Essay Concerning Human Understanding,* when the transition from mercantile economy to industrialisation was taking place in England after the "Glorious Revolution" of 1688. Although Locke completed his work as early as in 1679, for some unknown reasons its publication was delayed until 1690. Locke anticipated the changes that were going to take place in England and put forward a theory of knowledge that suited the new socio-economic order. The new socio-economic order (industrialised society) required the development of experimental science in order to boost the industrial growth in England. Therefore, a theory of knowledge which is based on "experience" was absolutely necessary. This is precisely the task accomplished by Locke in opposition to continental rationalism.[4] Robert Boyle (1627-92) and Isaac Newton (1642-1727), the two great natural scientists and friends of Locke, inspired and influenced him to come out with a view that our ideas without any exception are grounded in sense-experience. This view of Locke, in a way, is a turning-point for the development of modern science. Much before Locke's realisation, it was Francis Bacon (1561-1626), the well-known British philosopher-scientist, who advocated the view that modern philosophy must be based on a new method of "observation." Such a method, explained Bacon, would not only unravel the secrets of Nature but also dispel the myths of traditionalism or speculative thinking prevalent in earlier systems. However, Locke's supposedly systematic presentation of empiricism earned him the title "the pioneer of British empiricism."

Locke's modest claim in his *An Essay Concerning Human Understanding* was to undertake the job of cleaning all the junk that stands in the way of knowledge and to "inquire into the

4. Maurice Cornforth, *Science and Idealism* (New York, 1947) and also see George Novack, *Empiricism and its Evolution* (New York, 1973).

original, certainty, and extent of *human knowledge* together with the grounds and degrees of *belief, opinion* and *assent* . . ..".[5] In order to achieve this goal Locke, first of all, launched a scathing attack on the doctrine of innate ideas.

The Doctrine of Innate Ideas

Locke views that some people are of the opinion that there are certain innate principles which "were stamped upon the mind of man, which the soul receives in its very first being, and brings into the world with it."[6] Although Locke did not make it explicit, it is implied that his tirade was against the continental rationalists in general and Descartes in particular. Even the great philosophers of antiquity such as Plato and St Augustine advanced the doctrine of innate ideas. Their epistemology is centred around this doctrine. In an attempt to discredit this doctrine, Locke classifies these ideas into two categories — mathematical and logical principles, and practical principles (moral rules). He argues that it is commonly held that since these principles are innate they command universal assent. But this is not true because:

> all children and idiots have not the least apprehension or thought of them. And the want of that is enough to destroy that universal assent which must needs be the necessary concomitant of all innate truths; it seems to me near contradiction to say that they are truths imprinted on the soul, which it perceives or understands not; imprinting, if it signifies anything, being nothing else but the making of certain truths to be perceived. For, to imprint anything on the mind without mind's perceiving it seems to me hardly intelligible. If therefore children and idiots have souls, have minds with those impressions upon them, they must

5. John Locke, *An Essay Concerning Human Understanding*, ed. with an introduction by A.D. Wooziey (Glasgow, 1977), p. 63.

6. Ibid., p. 67.

> unavoidably perceive them, and necessarily know and assent to those truths; which since they do not, it is evident that there are no such impressions.[7]

The above argument of Locke sounds reasonable; since it is evident from our own experience that children and savages do not know what the general truths are. It is only through experience they come to know about mathematics or logic or morals. Apart from that, it is important to note that universality (necessity), does not entail innateness. For example, the truths of mathematics and logic are necessary and universal. This does not mean that they are innate. Locke maintains that it is absurd that mind has all the innate ideas imprinted on it. If it were so, everyone of us must be a good mathematician and logician, and also a theist. Contrary to this view, we find people who are weak in mathematics and logic, and atheists. Further Locke argues, moral principles are not self-evident as they require proof, for they are not universal. To put it in the words of Locke:

> . . . there cannot any one moral rule be proposed whereof a man may not justly demand a reason; which would be perfectly ridiculous and absurd if they were innate, or so much as self-evident; which every innate principle must needs be, and not need any proof to ascertain its truth, not want any reason to gain its approbation.[8]

Locke does not admit any moral principle which is self-evidently true, for all moral principles require proof and justification. Thus, Locke rejects that doctrine of innate ideas. By denying the view that all knowledge is derived from some inner light, Locke is partly successful in clearing the junk that stands in the way of knowledge. Now it is his turn to put forth his own account of knowledge.

7. John Locke, op. cit., p. 68.

8. Ibid., p. 79.

Theory of Knowledge

Locke's psychological account of the theory of ideas is the basis for his epistemology. His claim that all our ideas originate in sense-experience, and these ideas serve as the building blocks for the construction of human knowledge is considered to be the basic tenet of empiricism. Locke defines an idea, with a view to elaborate his theory of ideas, as:

> . . . whatsoever is the object of the understanding when a man thinks. . . . Used it (idea) to express whatever is meant by phantasm, notion, species, or whatever it is which mind can be employed about in thinking.[9]

Then an idea, for Locke, can be anything that is employed by mind in the process of thinking irrespective of its source. These ideas, says Locke, ". . . are those expressed by the words 'whiteness,' 'hardness,' 'sweetness,' 'thinking,' 'motion,' 'man,' 'elephant,' 'army,' 'drunkenness,' and others. . . ."[10] This follows that every idea in the mind has a corresponding word to express it. This view of Locke is popularly known as ideational theory of meaning. To quote Locke here: "The use, then, of words is to be sensible marks of idea; and the ideas they stand for are their proper and immediate signification."[11] The ideational theory of Locke has played a key role in the philosophy of language in the early twentieth century in Britain and elsewhere in Europe.

As regards human mind, Locke holds that human mind in the beginning is a blank sheet of paper (*tabula rasa*) upon which impressions (ideas) are imprinted later on. Locke writes: "Let us then suppose the mind to be, as we say, white paper, void of all characters, without any ideas; how come it is to be

---

9. John Locke, op. cit., p. 66.
10. Ibid., p. 89.
11. Ibid., p. 259.

furnished? . . . To this I answer, in one word, from EXPERIENCE."[12] This experience is of two types — sensation and reflection. Those ideas, maintains Locke, produced by sensation are called sensible qualities such as yellow, white, heat, cold, soft, hard, bitter, sweet, etc. and "this great source of most of the ideas we have, depending wholly upon our senses, and derived by them to the understanding I call SENSATION."[13] Locke considers that sensation is the most important source of ideas. There are also ideas produced by the internal perception of the mind. They are "perception, thinking, doubting, believing, reasoning, knowing, willing, and all the different actings of our own minds; . . . This source of ideas every man has wholly in himself; and though it be not sense, as having nothing to do with external objects, yet it is very like it, and might properly enough be called internal sense. But as I call the other sensation, so I call this REFLECTION, . . ."[14] Reflection in Locke's view is the internal perception of psychical states.

The external material objects in the first place, states Locke, act on our mind to produce simple ideas. These ideas result directly from a single sense or from several senses simultaneously, from reflection or finally from the combination of sensation and reflection.[15] Mind with its own operations produces several complex ideas out of simple ideas. Hence, simple ideas are atoms, believes Locke, from which the whole complex of knowledge can be built; and these simple ideas supply materials for knowledge.

Operations of the Mind

Mind, then, for Locke, is a passive unit which simply receives

12. John Locke, op. cit., p. 89.
13. Ibid., p. 90.
14. Ibid.
15. Ibid., p. 101.

ideas and acts as a repository of all ideas. These ideas which are considered to be the raw materials or bedrocks of knowledge originate from sensation and reflection. Mind becomes active only when it starts producing complex ideas with the help of its own operations, namely, comparing, compounding and abstraction. Comparison is an act of mind that consists in bringing two distinct simple or complex ideas together by relating them. Compounding is a process through which mind "puts together several of those simple ones it has received from sensation and reflection, and combines them into complex ones."[16] The unity of simple ideas into complex ones is truly a mental activity. Of all the three notable operations of mind, abstraction is an important activity. Locke holds that all our scientific knowledge is based on abstract general ideas. These abstract general ideas are the outcome of the mental abstraction. In order to form the abstract general ideas "the mind makes the particular ideas received from particular objects to become general; which is done by considering them as they are in the mind, such appearances, separate from all other existence, and the circumstances of real existence, as time, place, or any other concomitant ideas."[17] Thus, generality or universality of certain ideas is abstracted by the mind only when it comes into contact with several particular objects. For example, "whiteness" is a general abstract idea; such an idea is seen in all the white objects like snow, milk, etc. The notion that universal features are abstracts from particular existents shows us that Locke is a nominalist.

By recognising the operations of human mind, Locke makes it very clear that mere simple ideas produced by sensation and reflection are of no use without mind's participation in the production of various complex ideas. In this way Locke gives

---

16. John Locke, op. cit., p. 128.

17. Ibid., p. 129.

due importance to the powers of human mind.[18] Although mind can know only its ideas, yet Locke maintains that ideas are caused by external material objects. He argues: "it is evident the mind knows not things immediately, but only by the intervention of the ideas it has of them. Our knowledge, therefore, is real only so far as there is conformity between our ideas and the reality of things."[19] From the above statement of Locke we can infer that Locke is not only an empiricist but also a realist because of his admission that there are objects external to the perceiving mind. The knowledge of those external objects is not directly given to the perceiving mind but through the medium of ideas. In other words, ideas are the copies of external objects. Thus Locke advocates the doctrine of representationalism.

Primary and Secondary Qualities

Locke makes a sharp distinction between "ideas" and "qualities." He writes in his *Essay*: "whatsoever the mind perceived in itself, or is the immediate object of perception, thought, or understanding, that I call idea; and the power to produce any idea in our mind I call quality of the subject wherein that power is."[20] It logically follows that if qualities have power to produce ideas in our mind then what we call an object is nothing but a sum total of its qualities. According to Locke, there are two types of quality. They are:

> Qualities thus considered in bodies are . . . utterly inseparable from the body, in whatsoever state it be; . . . These I call original or primary qualities of body, which I think we may observe to produce simple ideas in us, viz. solidity, extension, figure

18. Similar view was expressed hy Immanuel Kant in his major work *Critique of Pure Reason*. Kant felt that mere sensory data (material element) without the categories of understanding do not give genuine knowledge of the reality.
19. John Locke, *An Essay Concerning Human Understanding*, p. 348.
20. Ibid., pp. 111-12.

> motion or rest and number. Secondly, such qualities which in truth are nothing in the objects themselves but powers to produce various sensations in us by their primary qualities, i.e. by the bulk, figure, texture, and motion of their insensible parts, as colours, sound, tastes. These I call secondary qualities.[21]

Locke, thus, distinguishes among simple ideas those which have objective significance from those which have mere subjective significance. The former he calls simple ideas of primary qualities (extension, figure, motion or rest and number) and the latter simple ideas of secondary qualities (colour, odour, taste, sound, etc.). Primary qualities are inseparable from the bodies (substances). A body (substance) ceases to be a body if any one of the primary qualities is missing in it. In other words, none of the primary qualities listed above can exist in isolation from the other qualities. Maybe this is the reason why Locke accorded primary status to them; while the secondary qualities are dependent upon primary qualities for their existence. Locke holds that our ideas of secondary qualities vary according to percipient's psychical states. Thus, they are subjective and relative. Apart from that, one can imagine a substance without secondary qualities, but one cannot do so without primary qualities. For example, according to scientists, water (H_2O) as a substance does not have colour, taste, smell, etc. But this cannot be a valid reason to say that they are not objective at all. If like the ideas of secondary qualities, the ideas of primary qualities are also given in sense perception what guarantee do we have to say that they (ideas of primary qualities) exactly resemble the objects? On the one hand, Locke advocates representative theory of perception in so far as the ideas of primary qualities represent objects as they are; on the other hand, his causal theory of perception suggests that ideas are caused by the objects that exist external to us.

21. John Locke, op. cit., p. 112.

What is Knowledge?

In order to explicate his epistemological position, Locke states as follows:

> Since the mind in all its thoughts and reasonings hath no other immediate object but its own ideas, which it alone can contemplate. It is evident that our knowledge is only conversant about them. . . . Knowledge then seems to me to be nothing but the perception of the connexion and agreement, or disagreement and repugnancy of any of our ideas. In this alone it consists.[22]

From the above statement of Locke, we can deduce that when we are engaged in any cognitive activity such as perception, thought, understanding, and judgement, the objects of cognition are not objects existing independent of the human mind but are our own ideas. Perhaps, in Locke's view, they are the ideas and supplied by the objects outside us when our sensations act upon them. Mind, then, arranges and rearranges these ideas with a view to match them with the external objects perceived through senses. In fact, Locke's account of knowledge leads us to epistemological dualism, namely, (a) coherence theory of ideas and (b) correspondence theory of ideas. If knowledge is derived from the agreement and disagreement of ideas, then there is no possibility of going beyond them, and knowing their correspondence to reality. Thus we are only left with ideas of things and not with the things themselves. But, Locke maintains that ideas are the copies of the objects external to us. This view of Locke establishes that there is a correspondence between the ideas and what they are ideas of. However, Locke's conception of knowledge limits the scope of knowledge of things, since all our ideas are not copies of objects, excepting the ideas of primary qualities.

---

22. John Locke, op. cit., p. 320.

Levels of Human Knowledge

Locke's undaunted attempt to explain the dispositional character of human knowledge is seen in his classification of knowledge into intuitive, demonstrative and sensitive forms. Intuitive knowledge, for Locke, is the most clear and certain. Such knowledge comes to human mind like a flash without the intervention of any other ideas. We can establish our own existence with this form of knowledge. This is the highest form of knowledge, according to Locke, which human mind is capable of obtaining. In this regard Locke shares with Descartes that intuitive knowledge is indubitable. Unlike intuitive knowledge, demonstrative knowledge is the perception of agreement or disagreement of two ideas by the mediation of or intervention of other ideas.[23] In other words, it involves reasoning. For example, *A* is equivalent to *B*, because *A* and *B* are equivalent to *C*. We can express this proposition in the following manner:

$$A = C \text{ and } C = B; \text{ therefore, } A = B$$

The knowledge obtained through demonstration is as certain and clear as intuitive knowledge but not immediate. Locke tries to extend this method of demonstration to prove the existence of God and to establish the moral principles. The "knowledge" which is not clear and certain, asserts Locke, is not knowledge at all but a mere opinion. It only passes under the title "knowledge." It is surprising that Locke being a professed empiricist places sensitive knowledge under this category. To quote Locke:

> There is, indeed, another perception of the mind employed about the particular existence of finite beings without us; which, going beyond bare probability, and yet not reaching perfectly to either of the foregoing degrees of certainty, passes under the name "knowledge."[24]

23. John Locke, op. cit., pp. 325-29.

24. Ibid., p. 330.

This knowledge of the existence of the particular objects is called sensitive knowledge. Locke says that there is no element of certainty in this kind of knowledge. In spite of his claim that all knowledge comes through sense-experience alone, Locke could not justify his claim by reducing sensitive knowledge to mere opinion.

What is Substance?

Locke attempts to deduce the existence of substance from the awareness of ideas. He advances the view that when we repeatedly find a group of simple ideas associated together, "We accustom ourselves to suppose some substratum wherein they do subsist, and from which they result, which therefore we call substances."[25] Though Locke could establish the existence of substance with the help of simple ideas, yet he holds that the nature of substance is something mysterious that he "knew not what."[26] Locke argues that our ideas do not inform anything about the nature of substance: they only indicate to us that substances do exist, which are ultimate causes of our own ideas. Locke maintains "that the idea of corporeal substance in matter is as remote from our conceptions and apprehensions as that of spiritual substance, or spirit."[27] It implies that we must forever remain ignorant of the nature of substance in any from.

To be consistent with his empiricism, Locke argues that all that we can know are ideas of qualities. Behind these qualities there must be something which bears all these qualities. Thus we can, according to Locke, infer the existence of substance from these ideas of qualities, but we do not have any access to know its nature. It amounts to saying that for Locke qualities

---

25. John Locke, op. cit., p. 185.
26. Ibid., p. 186.
27. Ibid., p. 187.

do not really constitute the nature of substance. They are only the representations of substance, but not the very constitutive aspects of it. This view of Locke is akin to Kant's "thing-in-itself."

Language: means of exchanging views

Locke's views on language are inextricably linked up with his view that there are abstract general ideas. Language is an instrument through which humans in society exchange their views or thoughts or ideas with their fellow beings. By God's grace, says Locke, men have been endowed with the power of articulation. As we all know, words play the key role in language. These words are sensible signs. In other words, words represent ideas in the mind. To put it in Locke's language:

> The comfort and advantage of society not being to be had without communication of thoughts; it was necessary that men should find out some external sensible signs, where of those invisible ideas, which his thoughts are made up of, might be known to others. For this purpose nothing was so fit, either for plenty or quickness, as those articulate sounds, with so much ease and variety he found himself able to make. Thus we may conceive how words, which were by nature as well adapted to that purpose, came to be made use of by men as the signs of their ideas; not by any natural connection that there is between articulate sounds and certain ideas, for then there would be but one language amongst all men. . . .[28]

In line with his empiricism, Locke maintains that there is a connection between words and ideas, but not between words and things. This connection is not a natural one. His empiricism forbids him to show any connection between words and things or objects since objects are never given in sensory experience directly. This theory of Locke is known as ideational theory.

28. John Locke, *An Essay Concerning Human Understanding*, p. 259.

In order to simplify language and to make it more effective form of communication among men, Locke felt the need of abstract general terms. What Locke believes is that there are several particular existents, and it is difficult to give name to each and every existent, since "it is beyond the power of human capacity to frame and retain distinct ideas of all particular things we meet with. . . ."[29] Then the only way out of the problem is to abstract the ideas from the particular existents so that an abstract idea stands for a class of things or properties or qualities, etc. For example, the concept (abstract idea) "man" stands for all those individuals who possess the essential quality of "humanness." The words, then, that signify or represent the abstract general ideas are general words (concepts). This is how, according to Locke, a proper communication network can be built up for the comfort of the society.

Long before the linguistic philosophers of the present century, Locke envisaged that linguistic errors (misuse of words) cause philosophical ambiguities. He laments that we tend to use certain words without knowing their proper meaning. This linguistic jugglery often leads us to philosophical aberrations. For instance, argues Locke, the words "wisdom," "glory," "grace" etc. are used by individuals, yet when one asks them for the meaning of those words, there would be no definite answer from them.[30] The most insistent abuse of words, according to Locke, is to reach the extreme conclusion that words stand for things. In support of his view Locke cites some examples from Aristotle and other Greek philosophers. Locke maintains that when Aristotle referred to the terms like "substantial forms," "vegetative souls;" "active reason," etc. he (Aristotle) might have thought that these words stand for certain things in reality; but these are concepts of

29. John Locke, op. cit., p. 263.

30. Ibid., pp. 306-8.

metaphysics, which have no real existence. Not only the concepts of metaphysics, for that matter, but also the concepts that are used to refer to real existents do not stand for things. The reason is that words stand for ideas. Thus, Locke suggests to us that we should not employ ambiguous words in our language to avoid intellectual regression.

There is no doubt that Locke has provided us with a neat analysis of use and abuse of words. By and large, his arguments in favour of the need of abstract general ideas for the development of language and his crusade against the misuse of words are worthy enough to be considered. But the fundamental flaw in Locke's analysis springs from his denial of the view that words stand for things. It is true that certain words that are used in our normal course of conversation do not stand for anything in reality. None the less, it is not true that all the words are of the same kind. For instance, when we teach children the meanings of words, we point out to things but not to ideas. If a child wants to know "what does a horse mean?" we normally show child a picture of a horse or a real one. Thus, some words have direct connection with things. If what Locke proposes were true then we have to point out to an idea of horse to explain the meaning of the term "horse." But ideas cannot be pointed out to. In that case a child cannot attach meaning to anything since no one taught the child "what it really means" In so far as the reality of things is concerned, words derive meanings from the objects but not from ideas. However, as pointed out by Locke, there are certain words like "glory," "grace," and "God" which do not stand for anything in reality, but they are used in our day-to-day language. Perhaps such words derive their meanings from the actions of the individuals. Such "things" can never be pointed out. They are not visible but are intelligible.

To conclude, Locke's epistemology on the whole suffers from lack of cogency, consistency and proper direction. Locke started with a modest claim that all our knowledge without exception is grounded in sense-experience, but went on to show that knowledge derived through sense-experience is most uncertain and only probable. Another notable inconsistency in Locke's epistemology consists in his classification of simple ideas into ideas of primary qualities and ideas of secondary qualities. This distinction sounds reasonable so long as their subsistence in the object is concerned. As explained earlier, certain qualities have been accorded primary status because a substance ceases to be a substance if any one of those qualities is missing in it. But the existence of secondary qualities in the object is only optional in the sense that the substance may possess secondary qualities or may not possess them at all. The non-possession of secondary qualities does not deprive substance of its identity. The problem arises only when Locke assigns objective and absolute status to primary qualities, and subjective and relative status to secondary qualities. As we know, for Locke, both the ideas of primary qualities and the ideas of secondary qualities are given in sense-experience, then why the same sense-experience could tell us that one set of qualities is objective and other set is mere subjective? There is no rationale behind it. Another inconsistency in Locke's epistemology is that in spite of the fact that qualities exist in the substance and its existence is established through the ideas of these qualities (primary qualities), Locke declares that the nature of substance (substratum) is not known as if qualities have a separate existence from the substance. If all that human mind knows is its own ideas, then what justification does Locke have to give that there are objects external to us? These are some of the glaring contradictions in Locke's epistemology. This very inconsistent philosophy of Locke paves the way for the subjective idealist philosophy of Berkeley.

GEORGE BERKELEY (1685-1753)

Taking the cue from John Locke that all genuine knowledge

invariably comes through sense-experience, Berkeley sets out to rectify the mistakes committed by Locke with a view to systematising empiricism. His chief mission in his work, *The Principles of Human Knowledge,* is, on the one hand, to show that things exist in so far as they are perceived, and on the other hand, to disprove the belief in the existence of matter. Berkeley being the Bishop of Clione sees to it that his empiricism does not dispel the claim that God exists; instead he tries to prove the existence of God with his patent formula *esse est percipi*. Being a man of religious fervour, Berkeley does not want science to dominate the scene in explaining the nature of reality in terms of matter and motion as explained by the Newtonian physics. However, he claims that his motive is not to deprive science of its proper place but to shape his philosophy in accordance with common-sense viewpoint. In an attempt to provide a common-sense view of reality, Berkeley converts empiricism into subjective idealism by refusing to grant independent status to reality. Another feature of Berkeley's philosophy is to reconcile science with religion in order to maintain the view that science and religion are properly balanced. Let us examine the important aspects of Berkeley's epistemology.

Ideas as the Objects of Knowledge

Like his predecessor (empiricist predecessor) John Locke, Berkeley defines an idea as "the immediate object of sense or understanding."[31] Though Berkeley did not make it clear what he really meant by understanding, later in his *Principles* he tries to explain understanding in terms of perception.[32] He recognises three types of idea. They are:

---

31. George Berkeley, *The New Theory of Vision*, section 45.
32. George Berkeley, *The Principles of Human Knowledge,* ed. with an introduction by G.J. Warnock (Glasgow, 1977), p. 77.

> . . . ideas actually imprinted on the senses; or else such as are perceived by attending to the passions and operations of the mind; or lastly, ideas formed by help of memory and imagination either compounding, dividing, or barely representing those originally perceived in aforesaid ways.[33]

What Berkeley wants to convey is that ideas of sense supply us with the qualities like taste, smell, hot, cold, figure or size, etc. These ideas are of sensible qualities. The ideas derived from passions and operations of mind (psychical states of human mind) are love, sympathy, and hatred. The ideas of memory are mere recollections of those ideas that have already been experienced. Ideas of imagination are products of human mind. They may even be fantasies. All these ideas derived through the aforesaid three ways, claims Berkeley, are the objects of human knowledge.

Now the question before Berkeley is: Where do these ideas exist? For ideas to exist there must be something that can contain all these ideas. Berkeley believes: ". . . there is . . . something which knows or perceives them (ideas) and exercises diverse operations as willing, imagining, and remembering about them. This perceiving active being is what I call Mind, Spirit, Soul or Myself."[34] Like Descartes and Locke, Berkeley too believes that there must be a thing that can perceive, will, imagine and remember. Such a thing is what Berkeley calls Mind or Spirit or Soul or Myself. Thus Berkeley makes it clear that objects of our knowledge are ideas and those ideas exist in Mind or Spirit. Till this point we do not think that Berkeley has gone against Locke since both the philosophers accept the view that ideas are the objects of human knowledge and these ideas exist in Mind. The point of departure is that unlike Locke, Berkeley asserts that ideas are not the copies of objects, but objects are

33. George Berkeley, *The Principles of Human Knowledge*, p. 65.

34. Ibid.

collections of ideas. In this way, his position deviates from the representative theory of perception advocated by John Locke. It will be expounded in due course.

To be is to be Perceived (*Esse est percipi*)

Having arrived at the conception that ideas exist in mind or spirit, Berkeley argues that objects (sensible things) exist in so far as they are perceived. This slogan becomes central to Berkeley's empiricism. To quote Berkeley in this context:

> The table I write on, I say, exists, that is, I see and feel it; and if I were out of my study I should say it existed — meaning thereby that if I was in my study I might perceive it, or that some other spirit actually does perceive it. There was an odour, that is, it was smelt, there was a sound, that is, it was heard; a colour or figure, and it was perceived by sight or touch. This is all that I can understand by these and the like expressions.[35]

What follows from the above important argument of Berkeley is that objects exist in so far as they are perceived by minds. The term "exist" is inextricably linked up with perception. In other words, to exist is to be perceived. Berkeley elaborates this point by arguing that "the table in my room exists because I perceive it. That does not mean," says Berkeley, "that I take away its existence when I am out of my study." In line with common-sense viewpoint Berkeley argues that the table still exists in his study even when he is out of his study because some other spirit must be perceiving it. Thus Berkeley establishes existence of the over-vigilant Mind or Spirit with his *esse est percipi*. This ever-vigilant Mind or Spirit (God) forms the very nucleus of Berkeley's philosophy.

True to his expectations, Berkeley's *esse est percipi* makes empiricism more rigorous and consistent by dispelling atheism,

35. George Berkeley, *The Principles of Human Knowledge*, p. 66.

scepticism and solipsism. God being an Infinite Spirit keeps a constant vigil on the world of sensible things. Berkeley reaches his ontology through his epistemology. What is remarkable in Berkeley's philosophy is his bold attempt to prove the existence of God with his empiricist principle: "to be is to be perceived." If this principle is taken as a criterion to judge the existence of anything then God should not exist since He is imperceptible. But this conclusion would not have been palatable to Berkeley. He is clever enough to manage the whole issue. He starts with the existence of finite things and then reached the existence of Infinite God or Spirit. Unlike Locke, Berkeley does not give scope to scepticism in his philosophy. His anti-sceptical view saved him from all the dangers. Had he employed scepticism he could not have proved the existence of God with his empiricist principle *esse est percipi*. His logic is very simple. For an object to exist is to be perceived. He does not want to commit to the view that objects do not exist when no one perceives them. They do exist unperceived by finite minds. A sceptic might argue, what guarantee Berkeley can give that things exist even when no one perceives them. But Berkeley meticulously approaches this problem by saying that common sense tells us. Berkeley does not stop with that since he has committed to the principle that objects exist only in so far as they are perceived. In support of his thesis Berkeley goes on to tell that there is some Infinite Spirit or Mind which perceives them all through. Not only that, the principle *esse est percipi* disproves solipsism by recognising finite minds and Infinite Mind.

The view that objects for their existence are dependent upon the mind leads to subjective idealism. All the same, Berkeley's insistence on the view that reality for its existence is dependent on God's mind reduces Berkeley's position to objective idealism. Thus Berkeley's position oscillates between subjective and objective idealism.

Finite and Infinite Spirits

According to Berkeley, there are finite spirits and an Infinite Spirit. Ideas, in fact, subsist in these spirits. Spirits "are active, indivisible substances," whereas the "ideas are inert, fleeting, or dependent beings, which subsist not by themselves, but are supported by, or exist in minds or spiritual substances."[36] A spirit, for Berkeley, is a simple, active substance that can activate and support ideas. Berkeley maintains that ideas potentially exist in God's mind but actually exist in the finite minds or spirits. He opines:

> We perceive a continual succession of ideas; some are anew excited, others are changed or totally disappear. There is therefore some cause of these ideas, whereon they depend, and which produces and changes them. That this cause cannot be any quality, or idea, or combination of ideas is clear. . . . It must therefore be a substance . . . it remains therefore that the cause of ideas is an incorporeal active substance or spirit.[37]

In an attempt to vindicate the existence of God, Berkeley argues:

> Sensible things do really exist; and if they really exist, they are necessarily perceived by an Infinite Mind, therefore, there is an Infinite mind, or God. This furnishes you with a direct and immediate demonstration from a most evident principle of the being of a God.[38]

The argument put forward by Berkeley to prove the existence of God resembles the causal argument, according to which the world is a mere effect of an efficient cause called God or Creator. However, the question before Berkeley is: How does one know that there are spirits? Berkeley answers: "We may be said to have some knowledge or notion of our own minds, of spirits

36. George Berkeley, *The Principles of Human Knowledge,* p. 109.
37. Ibid., p. 77.
38. Ibid., p. 198.

and active beings — whereof in a strict sense we have not ideas."[39] But Berkeley nowhere provides any definition of the term "direct notion."

It is evident from Berkeley's account of spirits that there are ideas and spirits, in which these ideas exist or subsist. Finite spiritual substances (human minds) are the channels through which God operates everything in this world. He is the ultimate or prime cause of the reality of things. Thus Berkeley was successful in establishing the existence of God.

Immaterialism

Berkeley is allergic to the term "matter." He feels that Locke's empiricism is inconsistent because of his acceptance of the existence of material substance. Matter, for Berkeley, is ridden with internal contradictions and useless in the quest for knowledge. In order to refute the view that matter exists, Berkeley employs his own logic. He believes that idea of matter is an abstract idea. Controverting the views of Locke, Berkeley asserts that there are no abstract ideas. Being a nominalist like Locke, Berkeley accepts the existence of individual, simple sensible things or qualities. He maintains that knowledge consists of ideas of sensible qualities derived from senses. Berkeley holds that senses do not provide us with any abstract ideas. Hence, there are no abstract ideas. In an attempt to prove that material substance is an abstract idea, Berkeley argues:

> Let it be considered sensible qualities are colour, figure, motion, smell, taste, etc., i.e. the ideas perceived by sense. Now, for an idea to exist in an unperceiving thing is a manifest contradiction: for to have an idea is all one has to perceive; that therefore wherein colour, figure, etc. exist must perceive them; hence it is clear there can be no unthinking substance or substratum of those ideas.[40]

---

39. George Berkeley, *The Principles of Human Knowledge*, p. 109.
40. Ibid., p. 68.

What follows from that statement of Berkeley is that the idea of matter is purely a mental abstraction.

Proceeding further, Berkeley contests that what we call objects are nothing but collections of ideas or sensible qualities. He opposes Locke's distinction of primary and secondary qualities. A quality, according to Berkeley, is a sensible thing. All qualities are alike in their nature in the sense that they are effects produced by objects on our minds. They do not resemble the objects because of phenomenal variability. Therefore, the primary qualities (solidity, extension, figure, number, motion or rest) are as subjective as secondary qualities (colour, taste, smell, sound and touch). In his famous dialogues between Hylas and Phelonous, Berkeley argues as follows: The sensible qualities like heat and cold, sweet and bitter cannot exist without perceiving minds. For instance, heat cannot be in the objects but in our own minds. When a person touches a hot thing, he feels the sensation of heat. Such a sensation exists in his mind not in the objects. Similarly, all other sensible qualities like extension, figure, motion, etc. are sensible qualities existing in our minds not in the objects. They are all sensible qualities because they are sensed by perceiving minds. Thus Berkeley sums up, besides spirits all that we know or conceive are our own ideas.

What we can infer from the above argument of Berkeley is that his position ultimately boils down to phenomenalism; for he considers that all the objects are nothing but sensible qualities. These qualities are mind-dependent, consequently the objects which are composed of these sensible qualities are also mental. In this way, Berkeley reduces the reality of things to one's own sensations. These arguments of Berkeley further paved the way for the demolishing of the concept of matter. It is evident that Berkeley doubts least the existence of those things (sensible things or qualities) imprinted on the senses. They really exist. For example, when we perceive an apple, the colour, taste, smell, size and shape of the apple are all sensible qualities. No one would say colour is matter, taste is matter, smell is matter, size is matter, shape is matter, etc. Then, when each sensible quality by itself is not matter how can all these sensible qualities produce something called matter? So, matter does not exist. To quote Berkeley in this context:

> I do not argue against the existence of any one thing that we can apprehend either by sense or reflection. That the things I see with my eyes and touch with my hands do exist, really exist, I make not the least question. The only thing whose existence we deny is that which philosophers call Matter or Corporeal Substance. And in doing of this there is no damage done to the rest of mankind, who, I dare say, will never miss it. The atheist indeed will want the colour of an empty name to support his impiety. . . .[41]

Berkeley makes use of empiricism in a very systematic way to uphold the view that belief in the reality of matter is an unwarranted act of blind faith and says: "If so, it shall seem good, use the word 'matter' in the same sense as other men use 'nothing'.[42] Thus Berkeley uses "nothing" as a correct synonym for the term "matter." As a matter of fact, the term "Real" is a misnomer because for Berkeley a thing cannot be real, it is only an idea in the mind.

To conclude, Berkeley's main objective is to make empiricism more rigorous and consistent. In order to achieve his goal, he presented *esse est percipi* as a criterion to judge the existence of objects. However, Berkeley scrupulously manages the issue that this very criterion would not go against his Christian faith, viz. God does exist. Instead, Berkeley proves the existence of God with his epistemology. Ideas, for Berkeley, are not the copies of objects but are produced by minds. These

41. George Berkeley, *The Principles of Human Knowledge*, p. 81.
42. Ibid., p. 104.

ideas are nothing but sensible qualities. They cannot have independent existence apart from perceiving minds (finite spirits). Apart from ideas, Berkeley recognises spiritual substances, viz. finite minds and Infinite Mind. Ideas potentially exist in God's mind but actually exist in human minds. In fact, it is God who operates everything. In this way, the view that all objects, which are conglomerations of sensible qualities, for their existence are dependent upon finite minds leads to subjective idealism. However, the view that all objects, including finite spirits, for their existence are dependent on God's mind leads to objective idealism. Thus Berkeley's position oscillates between subjective and objective forms of idealism. What is the status of objects in Berkeley's philosophy? Well, the objects are nothing but collections of sensible qualities. These sensible qualities do not exist apart from perceiving mind. This position of Berkeley is known as phenomenalism. Berkeley employs his own logic to eliminate matter. In line with his empiricist tenets, he argues that things that are not perceived by mind cannot exist. Matter is not a sensible quality. So matter does not exist.

What is wrong with Berkeley's philosophy is its denial of existence of reality of objects independent of perceiving minds. He could not distinguish knowledge from existence. Knowledge presupposes existence. We cannot be said to have knowledge of objects unless they have existence of their own. It could have been better if his patent formula "to be is to be perceived" is changed to "to know is to be perceived." It is ridiculous to say that things do not exist without perceiving minds. It amounts to saying that before scientists discovered planets and their motion, various elements and their properties, islands and landscapes there were nothing of that sort but only after their discovery they came into existence. As once pointed out by G.E. Moore: ". . . that trains only have wheels while they are in stations, on the ground that passengers cannot see wheels while they remain in the train."[43] The views advocated by Berkeley go against common-sense view.

So far as the qualities are concerned, all qualities, says Berkeley, are alike. Opposing Locke's distinction of primary and secondary qualities, Berkeley maintains that all qualities are sensible and they can exist only in a perceiving mind. Thus they are subjective. What we call objects are nothing but collections of sensible qualities. It implies that since there is nothing external to perceiving minds, all objects are very much dependent on perceiving minds. What led Berkeley to this obnoxious conclusion is that he could not distinguish ideas from qualities. Any common-sense theory will tell us that objects possess various qualities. These qualities produce ideas in our minds when they come into contact with sense organs. In this way, ideas to a greater extent are produced by external objects. To this extent Locke's approach is more in accordance with common-sense viewpoint than Berkeley's.

Regarding matter, Berkeley has a strong feeling that matter does not exist because it is not perceived by minds. If perception were the criterion for anything's existence then spirits, both finite and infinite, should not exist as they are not perceived by minds. But Berkeley defends the existence of spirits by saying that we have a "direct notion" of them. Thus the criterion *esse est percipi* is arbitrary. If one wants to disprove the existence of a particular object or an idea one can employ this formula. However, the existence of unperceived objects can be established, if one feels like, saying that we have a direct notion of them. If matter is an abstract idea, then the spiritual substance is also an abstract idea, since it is not perceived by minds. Berkeley makes use of his patent formula to suit his interests. This parochial, subjective, idealist and sensationalist philosophy

43. Cf. Bertrand Russell, *History of Western Philosophy* (London, 1946), p. 631.

of Berkeley gave rise to very sceptical philosophy of David Hume.

DAVID HUME (1711-76)

Endorsing the idealist empiricist principles set forth by Berkeley, Hume states that an adequate philosophical system must be built upon "perceptions" (sense-impressions). Finding fault with Berkeley, Hume declares that empiricism is still impure because of the existence of spiritual substance. A pure empiricism (pure sensationalism) is possible only when we do away with, claims Hume, substance in any form, viz. mental or material. Hume thus carries empiricism to its logical conclusion by holding that all that exist are sense-impressions. Then the reality is nothing but a stream of sense-impressions. Fully convinced with his stand on substances (mental and material), Hume sets out to oust metaphysics from the sphere of philosophy. Metaphysics for Hume is a doctrine without any meaning. It is of no use in pursuit of knowledge of reality. Unlike Berkeley, Hume employs scepticism with a view to introducing an appropriate scientific method in philosophy. However, his very sceptical and pluralistic empiricist philosophy shatters the very foundations of science by denying the necessary causal connections that are prevalent in Nature. Let us examine and evaluate some of the cardinal doctrines of Humean empiricism.

Perceptions, Impressions and Ideas

Perception in general is regarded as a process by which we come to know various aspects of reality. In its broader sense, perception can be understood as a mental as well as a sensuous activity. For example, mind can perceive certain ideas without the aid of sensory experience. Such perception can be, in Kantian sense, called pure perception. Otherwise, many philosophers tend to restrict the term "perception" to mere sensuous activity.

In order to explain the origin of our ideas, Hume starts his *Treatise* by explaining three important concepts, viz. perception, impression and idea. According to him:

> All the perceptions of the human mind resolve themselves into two distinct kinds, which I shall call impressions and ideas. The difference between these consists in the degrees of force and liveliness, with which they strike upon the mind, and make their way into our thought or consciousness. Those perceptions which enter with most force and violence, we may name impressions, and under this name I comprehend all our sensations, passions, and emotions, as they make their first appearance in the soul. By ideas I mean the faint images of these in thinking and reasoning; . . .[44]

What follows from the above passage of Hume is that the term "perception" stands for any given datum in the mind. Such perceptions are categorised into impressions and ideas. Impressions, says Hume, are vivid, lively and direct. They have emotional strength and absolute status. They are more authentic sensory units. On the contrary, the ideas are secondary or derivative. They are the faint images of the sense-impressions. In other words, ideas are the copies of the impressions that include images, memories and thoughts. There cannot be ideas without impressions. Hume thus envisages that the only contents of mind are perceptions (impressions and ideas).

Hume classifies impressions and ideas into simple and complex ones. He conceives that simple perceptions (impressions and ideas) can neither be distinguished nor be separated since they are simple units. While the complex perceptions (impressions and ideas) can be distinguished or separated into parts as they are complex units made of simple perceptions. For instance, the qualities like colour, taste, smell, etc. are all united together in an apple, they can be distinguished

44. David Hume, *A Treatise of Human Nature*, Book I, ed. with an introduction by D.G.C. Macnabb (Glasgow, 1975), p. 45.

from one another.[45] In support of pure sensationalism, Hume draws the following conclusion:

> We may observe that it is universally allowed by philosophers, and is besides pretty obvious of itself, that nothing is ever really present with the mind but its perceptions or impressions and ideas, and that external objects become known to us only by those perceptions they occasion. . . . Since nothing is ever present to the mind; it follows, that it is impossible for us so much as to conceive of or form an idea of anything specifically different from ideas and impressions. Let us fix our . . . imagination to the heavens, or to the utmost limits of the universe; we never really advance a step beyond ourselves, nor can conceive any kind of existence, but those perceptions, which have appeared in that narrow compass.[46]

It implies that, however hard we venture to get out of the limits of this world to reach heavens or other worlds, we will not be successful in our endeavours because of the limitations of the mind. All that mind can grasp is its own perceptions (impressions and ideas). Although mind can exercise its absolute freedom to capture the world of objects, yet its immediate contents of perception are impressions and ideas. Other than these perceptions there is nothing for mind to conceive.

According to Hume, mind has two important features besides the activity of grasping perceptions. They are memory and imagination. Ideas are produced by memory and imagination. The ideas produced by memory are more reliable and consistent with those impressions which mind has had earlier, while the ideas produced by imagination might lead us to error since they are the products of improper judgement of human mind.[47] Hume thus believes that ideas of imagination may not resemble the original impressions.

45. David Hume, op. cit., p. 46.

46. Ibid., pp. 113-14.

47. Ibid., p. 52.

Like Locke and Berkeley, Hume too is of the opinion that ideas exist in human mind. What then is the status of sense-impressions? Are they mental or material? To say that an idea is non-mental results in contradiction; but to say that impressions (sense-impressions) are neither mental nor material does not result in any contradiction. Hume considers that these sense-impressions are independent of any substance. They are neutral entities. These neutral elements constitute the very essence of reality. They constitute ontology for Hume.

Denial of Substance

We have shown that Berkeley denies the existence of substance in its material form but admits its existence in spiritual form. Unlike Berkeley, Hume does not give any room to the notion of substance, for he conceives that the existence of substance in any form (spiritual or material) would prove fatal to the basic tenets of empiricism. Hume makes use of Berkeley's arguments against matter to dispense with the very notion or idea of substance. As a hard core empiricist, Hume asserts that he does not deny the existence of any object that is given in sense-experience (sensation or reflection). The impressions of sensation, maintains Hume, are original impressions; while the impressions of reflection are secondary.[48] Regarding the existence of substance, asks Hume, does such substance come from the senses? He answers that our senses supply us only with specific qualities but not with a unique substratum. So the idea of substance cannot be derived from the impressions of sensation or reflection. Like Berkeley, Hume argues:

> If it be perceived by the eyes it must be a colour; if by the ears, a sound; if by the palate, a taste; and so of the other senses. But l believe none will assert that substance is either a colour, a sound, or a taste. The idea of substance must, therefore, be derived from an impression of reflection, if it really exists.

48. David Hume, op. cit., p. 51.

> But the impressions of reflection resolve themselves into our passions and emotions; none of which can possibly represent a substance.[49]

Hume argues that we cannot have a perfect idea of anything except a perception. A substance is entirely different from a perception. Proceeding further, Hume makes it clear:

> The idea of substance . . . is nothing but a collection of simple ideas, that are united by the imagination, and have a particular name assigned to them, by which we are able to recall, either to ourselves or others, that collection.[50]

This shows that substance, according to Hume, is derived from a group of simple ideas that are derived from imagination. Hume has made it clear that the ideas produced by imagination are the product of the improper judgement of mind. Hume makes use of Berkeley's criticism of Locke's notion of unknown and unknowable substance to arrive at this conclusion. This position of Hume may be termed as phenomenalism. It is this position where the complex impressions are reduced to simple impressions and ideas. That is to say, reality is reduced to sense-impressions.

Hume maintains that spirit or self, like material substance, is a non-entity. He believes that any attempt to understand the nature of self or spiritual substance involves sense-impressions. He claims:

> For my part, when I enter most intimately into what I call myself, I always stumble on some particular perception or other, of heat or cold, light or shade, love or hatred, pain or pleasure. I never can catch myself at any time without a perception, and never can observe anything but the perception.[51]

49. David Hume, op. cit., pp. 59-60.
50. Ibid., p. 60.
51. Ibid., pp. 301-2.

The self or spiritual substance, then, is nothing but a bundle of sense-impressions. We cannot talk about its unity and simplicity without perceptions. Thus Hume claims to have successfully dispensed with the notion of spiritual substance of Berkeley. But he needs to answer the questions: Who is the subject of experiences, if there is no substantive self? What is the status of a person in the absence of a continuous self? Hume's bundle of theories of self cannot rationally answer these questions.

Theory of Knowledge

Hume, after settling the issue about the ultimate constituents of reality, tries to elaborate his theory of knowledge. He classifies human knowledge into two kinds: (a) Relations of ideas and (b) Matters of fact. According to him,

> the relations of ideas . . . are the sciences of Geometry, Algebra, and Arithmetic and in short, every affirmation which is either intuitively or demonstratively certain. That the square of the hypotenuse is equal to the square of the two sides is a proposition which expresses a relation between these two figures. That three times five is equal to the half of thirty, expresses a relation between these numbers. Propositions of this kind are discoverable by the mere operation of thought, without dependence on what is anywhere existent in the universe. Though there never was a triangle in nature, the truths demonstrated by Euclid would forever retain their certainty and evidence.[52]

What is evident from the above statement is that Hume being a professed empiricist accepts a priori forms of knowledge. This class of propositions (relations of ideas) comprises statements of mathematics and logic. These statements are self-evidently true and are independent of sense-experience. For

52. David Hume, *An Enquiry Concerning Human Understanding*, in A.J. Ayer and R. Winch (eds.), *British Empirical Philosophers: Locke, Berkeley, Hume, Reid, and Mill* (New York, 1968), p. 504.

example, the proposition 3×5 = 15 expresses a relation between numbers. Since the values of these numbers are fixed, we can know for certain that this proposition is true without appealing to any experience. Hence, they can be worked out according to the laws of logical implication. Such propositions, says Hume, are universal and necessary. Their truths are indubitable. Like Descartes, Hume employs the method of intuition to arrive at the truths of mathematics. On the contrary, matters of fact, says Hume, are dependent upon experience (sense-experience). Unlike the relations of ideas, they are not universal and certain. To quote Hume in this context:

> Matters of fact, which are the second objects of human reason, are not ascertained in the same manner, nor is our evidence of their truth, however great, of a like nature with the foregoing. The contrary of every matter of fact is still possible; because it can never imply a contradiction, and is conceived by the mind with same facility and distinctness, as if ever so conformable to reality.[53]

Hume thus holds that all the matters of fact are highly probable. All knowledge of natural sciences falls under this category.

Prior to Hume, it was Gottfried Leibniz who made a sharp distinction between necessary and contingent truths. According to him, the necessary truths are based on the principles of identity and non-contradiction. These truths are also known as truths of reason. The contingent truths are based on sense-experience and are guided by the law of sufficient reason. Leibniz holds the view that the law of sufficient reason demands the "why" of things. It always requires explanation. Being a rationalist, Leibniz established that the truths of reason (necessary truths) are superior to truths of fact (contingent truths). Besides the terminological difference, the only difference between Leibniz and Hume is that Leibniz is a

53. David Hume, *An Enquiry Concerning Human Understanding*, p. 504

professed rationalist and Hume is a hard core empiricist. Subsequently, Kant in eighteenth century and logical positivists in twentieth century made a watertight distinction between analytic and synthetic propositions. However, Kant differs from Hume; while logical positivists accepted Hume's classification without any modification. This we shall discuss in due course.

Not contented with the mere classification of knowledge into relations of ideas and matters of fact, Hume proceeds further to cut short the unwanted elements that are prevalent in philosophy. He launches a crusade against transcendental metaphysics. Hume contends that speculative philosophy dominated the scene for a long time. Now it is the time to abandon such philosophical thinking in order to make philosophy a genuine branch of knowledge. Hume's distaste for metaphysics is seen in the following passage:

> When we run over libraries, persuaded of these principles, what havoc must we make? If we take in our hand any volume, of divinity or school metaphysics, for instance, let us ask, does it contain any abstract reasoning concerning quantity or number? No. Does it contain any experimental reasoning concerning matter of fact and existence? No. Commit it then to the flames; for it can contain nothing but sophistry and illusion.[54]

For Hume, any piece of information can be considered as knowledge in so far as it comes under either of these two categories, namely, relations of ideas or matters of fact. According to Hume, metaphysics does not comply with the conditions set forth by him. Therefore, metaphysics is nonsensical. It is of no use in the acquisition of knowledge of any form. His anti-metaphysical stance paved the way for a positivist thinking in philosophy.

---

54. David Hume, *An Enquiry Concerning Human Understanding*, p. 515.

Theory of Causation

Hume has given an incisive analysis of causation. Though it is discussed under a separate head, his theory of causation forms an important feature of his epistemology. Hume views that all the propositions of matters of fact (natural sciences) are derived from cause and effect relations. What, then, is this relation? Hume argues that it is the general feeling of the people to think that when two events have successive appearance, we tend to call the antecedent event a "cause" and the consequent an "effect." But what makes people to think in that line? In an attempt to answer this question, Hume claims that our idea of causation rests upon the information received from sense-experience but not from any other source like abstract reasoning or reflection. With a view to providing us with a lucid exposition of causation, Hume recognises seven types of philosophical relation. They are — resemblance, identity, relations of time and place, proportion in quantity or number, degrees in any quality, contrariety, and causation. Out of these seven philosophical relations, four relations, viz. resemblance, contrariety, degrees in quality, and proportions in quantity or number are dependent on ideas. These philosophical relations may be changed without any change in the ideas. The knowledge derived from such relations is most certain and universal. Whereas the relations of identity, space and time, and causation are dependent on sense experience.[55] Of the seven philosophical relations mentioned above, causation, says Hume, is of paramount importance for our present enquiry. Hume believes that the observations of identity and the relations of space and time reveal to us that mind cannot be beyond the limits of its immediate perceptions. Then it is only the idea of causation that supplies us with some knowledge of the relations that exist between objects. To quote Hume in this context:

---

55. David Hume, *A Treatise of Human Nature*, Book I, pp. 105-6.

> It is only causation, which produces such a connection, as to give us assurance from the existence or action of one object, that it was followed or preceded by any other existence or action. . . .[56]

The idea of causation gives rise to an idea that certain events produce another set of events. Hume contests that the very idea of causation is based upon three important aspects, namely, contiguity, succession in time and the idea of necessary connection. Hume opines:

> . . . that whatever objects are considered as causes or effects, are contiguous; and nothing can operate in a time or place, which is ever so little removed from those of its existence. Though distant objects may sometimes seem productive of each other, they are commonly found upon examination to be linked by a chain of causes, which are contiguous among themselves, and to the distant objects. . . . We may therefore consider the relation of contiguity as essential to that of causation. . . .[57]

Hume points out that it is the general tendency of the people to attribute some kind of relationship (causal) between two events that have contiguous existence. Such a relationship is apprehended by mind whenever it perceives two distant events, having contiguous existence. The second aspect that is essential, claims Hume, to establish causal link between two events is succession in time. If this aspect is not taken care of then there are no causes and effects. The supposed time-gap between events suggests to us that there is no co-existence among objects. Here Hume's usage of the term "co-existence" is to be interpreted as contemporaneity. Thus, for Hume, events have successive appearances in time. The third and most important aspect, according to Hume, which is supposed to be the cardinal aspect of causation, is the idea of necessary connection. But

56. David Hume, *A Treatise of Human Nature*, pp. 119-20.

57. Ibid., p. 121.

where does this idea of necessary connection come from? This question of Hume changes the entire theme of causation.

Hume argues that one can have perceptions of the relations of contiguity and succession in time but not the idea of necessary connection. He considers that the terms "efficacy," "agency," "power," "force," "energy," "necessity," "connection," and "productive quality" are one and the same but for terminological difference. Denying that these terms provide us any idea, Hume asks whether these terms are derived from any impressions. Ideas, says Hume, represent their objects (sense-impressions). As pointed out earlier there cannot be an idea without an impression. If there is one then it must be the product of imagination. Such an imaginary idea is a mere fantasy since it is the product of improper judgement of human mind.[58] The idea of necessary connection then is inferred from the relations of contiguity and succession in time. As such, claims Hume, there is nothing like necessary connection. Thus Hume declares:

> The idea of necessity arises from some impression. There is no impression conveyed by our senses which can give rise to that idea. It must, therefore, be derived from some internal impression, or impression of reflection. There is no internal impression which has any relation to the present business, but that propensity, which custom produces, to pass from an object to the idea of its usual attendent. This, therefore, is the essence of necessity. Upon the whole, necessity is something that exists in the mind, not in objects. . . .[59]

From the above quotation of Hume what we can understand is that there is no causal necessity between the events in nature. The idea of necessary connection is purely psychological and is based on custom and habit. The repeated occurrences of certain phenomena make us believe that there is a necessary causal connection between events but there is none.

58. David Hume, *A Treatise of Human Nature*, p. 208.

59. Ibid., pp. 216-17.

The intrigues and intricalities involved in Hume's theory of causation are many. By denying the necessary causal connection between the events in nature, Hume has done an irreparable damage to the foundations of science. This position of Hume leads to scepticism. We can never be certain on anything in this world. Consequently, all the propositions of natural sciences remain as mere probabilities. Though Hume appears to be consistent in his approach, his empiricism has been transformed into pure sensationalism. As a matter of fact, his ontology is construed in such a way that it does not give any scope for internal relations among the events of nature. If all that exist are fleeting, discrete sense-impressions, then there is no scope for any internal relationship among these atomic units which constitute the essence of reality. Unlike Cartesian doubting method, Hume's scepticism is purely psychological. Descartes' approach is methodological and is employed to arrive at certainty. On the contrary, Hume's scepticism is psychological and is employed to arrive at probable knowledge.

External World

Hume extends his scepticism to the existence of objects external to us. According to him, the view that objects external to us have a continuous existence is derived from two important factors, viz. constancy and coherence. As such, claims Hume, the senses, the only faculty on which we rely upon for any knowledge of reality, cannot guarantee the continuous existence of any object or objects. He holds that:

> For that is a contradiction in terms, and supposes that senses continue to operate, even after they have ceased all manner of operation. These faculties, therefore, if they have any influence in the present case, must produce the opinion of the distinct; not of a continued existence. . . .[60]

60. David Hume, *A Treatise of Human Nature*, pp. 239-40.

Hume employs a thoroughgoing scepticism to erase the idea from the minds of the people who think that objects have a continuous existence. The senses give us only a distinct idea of the object or objects perceived. Proceeding further, Hume asks: How then this idea of continuous and external existence or objects is arrived at? In an attempt to answer this question, Hume says that the idea of continuous and external existence of objects is derived from constancy and coherence that we see in nature. He argues:

> Those mountains, and houses, and trees, which lie at present under my eye, have always appeared to me in the same order; and when I lose sight of them by shutting my eyes or turning my head, I soon after find them to return upon me without the least alteration. . . . This is the case with all the impressions whose objects are supposed to have an external existence. . . .[61]

The belief that objects have a continuous and external existence is founded on the view that objects have a consistent appearance whenever we perceive them. For instance, the natural objects like mountains, trees, landscapes do not change their positions. The change in the positions can be attributed to the perceiver, but not to things of this sort. Similarly, coherence, believes Hume, is another aspect that supports constancy in establishing the view that objects have continuous external existence. There are certain things which are subjected to changes; these changes provide us with an idea of coherence. Hume tries to drive home his point with the following example:

> When I return to my chamber after an hour's absence. I find not my fire in the same situation in which I left it; but then I am accustomed, in other instances, to see a like alteration produced in a like time, whether I am present or absent, near or remote. This coherence, therefore, in their changes, is one

61. David Hume, *A Treatise of Human Nature*, pp. 245-46.

of the characteristics of external objects, as well as their constancy.[62]

The repeated occurrence of certain phenomena, holds Hume, is the important factor that gives rise to the idea of coherence. In turn this idea of coherence suggests to us that objects exist external to us even when they are not presented to the senses. In spite of these two important proofs which guarantee the independent and continued existence of objects, Hume being a sceptic goes on telling that these two proofs are not rational enough to justify the view that there is a world external to us. In this way, Hume's arguments against the existence of external world are more contentious rather than demonstrative. Hume's main interest proves to be one that cannot accommodate anything except perceptions.

To conclude, Hume appears to be more complacent than Locke and Berkeley by virtue of his claim that he has made empiricism more systematic and rigorous by dispelling the notion of substance in any form in order to establish the supremacy of sense-impressions. These supposedly neutral, lively, vivid, discrete atomic units constitute the essence of reality. In other words, reality is nothing but a stream of sense-impressions. Though human mind has got all the freedom to go round the universe, still it cannot grasp anything except a perception, which is immediate. All knowledge, excepting the knowledge of exact sciences, of reality is supplied by sense-impressions which are supposed to be authentic sources of information. However, the knowledge supplied by sense-impressions is not certain, but highly probable. Regarding causation, Hume says that there is no necessary causal connection between events. Our senses do not inform anything about such a connection. Mere temporal succession of events in reality gives rise to the idea of causation. As such the idea of causation is psychological and is derived from habit and custom.

62. David Hume, *A Treatise of Human Nature*, p. 246.

Being an ardent sceptic, Hume does not accept the independent and continuous existence of objects in reality. Objects are mere conglomerations of sense-impressions. By denying the necessary causal connection between events in nature, Hume doubts the very foundations of science. From a set of probabilities we can derive another set of probabilities. Science, then, is deprived of certainty and universality. All scientific formulations are derived from evanescent sense-impressions.

To sum up, the turn of empirical thought which started from Locke, through Berkeley to Hume reduces everything to sense-impression. As pointed out by Maurice Cornforth,[63] Locke identified three entities of being amongst the objects of knowledge, viz. (a) ideas, (b) the self or mind to which these ideas belong, and (c) material substance, which they represent. Whereas Berkeley reduces Locke's three entities into two, viz. (a) ideas and (b) spirits (infinite and finite) to which the ideas belong, finally, Hume reduces these two entities into one, viz. perceptions (impressions and ideas). They represent nothing. They have an independent existence. They are neither material nor mental. Reality is the sum total of these impressions. Thus Hume advocates pure phenomenalism. Berkeley and Hume abolished the distinction between appearance and reality. Whatever is given in sense perception is real. There is nothing real behind these appearances. Locke is an exception in this regard. He recognised something real behind these appearances, which he says that "I know not what it is."

In this exposition of the development of classical British empiricism, we have confined our discussion to the central issues of the epistemological doctrines of Locke, Berkeley and Hume. Some of the issues that are not pertinent to the present study have been omitted. The basic tenets of classical British empiricism have been adopted by logical positivists and are projected by them in a different linguistic garb.

63. Maurice Cornforth, *Science and Idealism* (New York, 1947), p. 55.

2

The Birth of Logical Positivism and its Objectives

LOGICAL positivism emerged as an influential philosophical thought between two world wars. A group of like-minded philosophers and scientists joined together to imbue scientific temper among philosophers. They felt that traditional philosophy was dominated by speculative thinking (metaphysics) that often led to absurd philosophical conclusions that stood in glaring contradiction to the results of modern science. They believed that the only panacea is to destroy the seeds of speculative thinking in order to make philosophy a genuine branch of human knowledge. Prima facie, the claim of logical positivists appears to be very sensible, but how far are they successful in their endeavour is altogether a different question. We are going to discuss this issue in detail in the succeeding chapters. Let us discuss the history of logical positivist movement and its objectives.

The Vienna Circle

What is known as logical positivism is the appellation given to the philosophical ideas of the Vienna Circle. The Circle came into existence in 1922 under the leadership of Moritz Schlick (1882-1936), Professor of Philosophy at Vienna. The members of the Circle belonged to different disciplines like philosophy, science, mathematics, and other social sciences. Although they belonged to different disciplines, they shared a common taste, namely, scientific temper. Schlick was chosen as the leader of the group because of his background in physics. He had close personal relations with the physicists like Max Plank, Albert Einstein, and Hilbert. In addition to that, Schlick had earned some reputation as a philosopher of science. Apart from Schlick, the other members of the Circle were Otto Neurath, a prominent member of the Circle and a social scientist, Friedrich Waismann, Herbert Feigl, Victor Kraft, Philip Frank, Karl Menger, Kurt Gödel and Hans Hahn. As a young student of philosophy A.J. Ayer associated himself with the Circle but was not a member of the Circle. In 1926 a prominent figure by name Rudolf Carnap (1891-1970) became a member of the Circle. On the one side Schlick and on the other side Carnap established themselves as two protagonists of the Circle. The group led by Schlick was known as "right wing" because of their moderate views on various issues; while the other group led by Carnap was known as "left wing" for their radical approach towards various issues. Before joining the Circle in 1926, Carnap worked independently on his own on the issues related to logic and science. In one of his personal letters Carnap writes as follows:

> Until 1926 I worked completely on my own in a small village in Germany. I started out on my philosophical road, strongly influenced by Russell and Frege (my teacher). My aim was the application of modern logic for the analysis of scientific concepts and the clarification of philosophical problems. I was not at all thinking of a philosophical movement. My early publications are concerned with topics in the foundations of physics (as was my Ph.D. thesis on space), a textbook on symbolic logic (stressing particularly its applications). The largest part of my time in these early years, however, was devoted to writing *Der Logische Aufbau der Welt;* the manuscript was finished when I came to Vienna in 1926.[1]

1. Cf. W.P. Alston and Nakhnikian (eds.), *Readings in Twentieth Century Philosophy* (London, 1963), p. 384.

Since then Carnap became an active member of the group. It appears that he was more interested in the problems of syntax rather than in the problems of semantics. Carnap's taste for syntax is seen in his work, *The Logical Syntax of Language*. Though Carnap claims that he was more influenced by Russell and Frege, there were many who said that the Vienna Circle received all inspiration from Wittgenstein (1889-1951). According to A.J. Ayer, the *Tractatus Logico-Philosophicus* of Wittgenstein has had a profound influence on the Vienna Circle.[2] But, Carnap was not in complete agreement with this statement. He feels that Wittgenstein's influence on the Vienna Circle is often exaggerated. To a greater extent, claims Carnap, Schlick and Waismann were influenced by Wittgenstein but not Neurath and himself.[3]

Having attracted circles of adherents in Vienna, Prague, Warsaw, Berlin, England and America, this movement claimed to engage in an analysis of the problems created by the development of modern science and aims at their logical analysis. Between 1922 and 1929, this movement gathered so much momentum that the members of the Circle used to have frequent philosophical deliberations. Though Wittgenstein and Karl Popper were not the members of the Circle, they used to take part in the deliberations of the Circle. In the meantime a similar but less influenced group surfaced in Berlin under the leadership of Hans Reichenbach. Both the groups shared their disliking for philosophers who have anti-scientific attitude. However, these groups worked independently. Ultimately in 1929, the members of the Circle felt that there was a need to identify themselves with a specific name and also to draft a definite programme of the group. They named their group "Vienna Circle" and also released a manifesto, *Scientific World*

2. A.J. Ayer, "Vienna Circle", *The Revolution in Philosophy*, p. 70.
3. Cf. W.P. Alston and Nakhnikian (eds.), *Readings in Twentieth Century Philosophy*, p. 384.

View: The Vienna Circle. In 1930, Rudolf Carnap and Hans Reichenbach jointly brought a journal under the title, *Erkenntnis*, to popularise the views of the Vienna Circle.

In 1931, the name "logical positivism" was coined by A.E. Blumberg and Herbert Feigl as a label for the philosophical views of the Vienna Circle. The term "positivism" is derived from Auguste Comte, Saint Simon, Ernst Mach and Karl Pearson for their anti-metaphysical stand and belief in the existence of positive facts; while "logical" is added because its exponents (the Vienna positivists) claim that their philosophy is confined to the logical analysis of everyday language and science. They also suggested alternative names such as "logical empiricism" and "scientific empiricism." They used empiricism because the members insisted that all our knowledge is confined to sense-experience. "Scientific" because they claim to hold the view that it is only in the sciences and by the use of "scientific method" that we can acquire knowledge about the physical world. However, Carnap and others preferred logical positivism as the right title to any other title. Thus logical positivists claim to stand for logical and scientific foundations of knowledge.

By 1936, the Circle lost its initial momentum and started disintegrating because of the various extraneous factors. Moritz Schlick, the important figure of the Circle, was shot dead by a demented student in 1933. After a year Hans Hahn, another important figure of the Circle, died. With the tragic deaths of two prominent figures, the Vienna Circle virtually became a non-entity and was dissolved. Apart from that, the Nazi aggression on Jewish community created terror among some of the members of the Circle. For fear of execution some of the members fled the country in search of better positions elsewhere. Gödel, Menger, Carnap, and Feigl fled to United States. Out of these Carnap was the last to die in the year 1970. F. Waismann joined the faculty at Oxford where he died in 1959.

Objectives of Logical Positivism

Logical positivists are supposed to have brought about a revolution in the circles of philosophy by showing their dissent against speculative thinking that is prevalent in traditional philosophies. According to logical positivists, the cardinal features of their philosophy are two: on the one hand to promote the reasoning concerning science and mathematics and on the other hand to oust metaphysics from the sphere of philosophy. Accordingly, the attention was given primarily to logical, epistemological and semantic issues. As a matter of fact, logical positivism is another form of empiricism. The adherents themselves claim that certain basic features of logical positivism resemble Humean empiricism. However, the only difference, according to logical positivists, between traditional empiricism of Hume and modern empiricism of logical positivists, lies in the latter's emphasis on a powerful logical technique. Thus "logical positivism, especially in the form of linguistic analysis, resembles classical British empiricism as a senile and impotent pedant resembles a lusty iconoclastic youth."[4]

Logical positivists assigned a special function to philosophy. As an enterprise, philosophy, supposed logical positivists, should undertake the business of clarifying the philosophical muddles that often appear due to loose correlation of our language. It is by no means a trivial business. Most of us realise:

> It is useful and necessary to eliminate unclarities and ambiguities from language to improve the functioning of that indispensable instrument of thought. But it is a paltry enterprise to convert this task into the paramount aim of philosophy.[5]

---

4. George Novack, *Empiricism and its Evolution*, p. 107.
5. Ibid., p. 108.

One can accept that it is one of the functions of philosophy but not as the only function of philosophy. As a matter of fact, this function (logical clarification of thought) deprives philosophy of any content. Thus, for logical positivists, philosophy is more an activity than a pedagogy with a definite subject matter.

One of the most important priorities of logical positivists is to eliminate metaphysics from philosophy. This attempt of logical positivists is not all that new in the history of philosophy. Prior to logical positivists, it was Hume who showed his distaste for metaphysics for it contains "nothing but sophistry and illusion." The French philosopher and socialist Auguste Comte felt that metaphysics is more concerned about impersonal and abstract forces of the phenomena. In that way it is dogmatic. Even Kant, the celebrated German philosopher, revealed that certain sort of metaphysics is impossible as the human understanding cannot reach the domains of metaphysics (thing-in-itself). Logical positivists made use of Hume's work to eliminate metaphysics.

In line with Humean arguments, logical positivists classified meaningful statements into two kinds: (a) analytic statements (relations of ideas in Humean terminology) of logic and mathematics, which do not require any confirmation from sense-experience for their certainty — in other words they are purely conventional and tautologous — and (b) synthetic statements (matters of fact in Humean terminology) of natural sciences, whose truth or falsehood is dependent on sense-experience. All those statements which do not fall under either of these two categories are metaphysical and consequently meaningless. In this way, they claim to demolish metaphysics completely. In order to judge the meaningfulness of a statement, logical positivists introduced "principle of verification" as a criterion of meaning by the use of which all the statements of science would be proved acceptable and metaphysics by contrast would be condemned as meaningless. All the analytic statements are exempted from this principle of verification since they are non-empirical.

Logical positivists hold the view that they are, as philosophers, not concerned with the truth or falsehood of scientific statements and assert that this is the business of scientists. They claim that their

> Proper concern is to enquire into the logical connections of the concepts and propositions of science, into how some propositions are deducible from others and the like. It is this kind of enquiry, the logical analysis of concepts, propositions, proofs, hypotheses, theories of science which constitute epistemology, indeed philosophy in general.[6]

It is evident from the above quotation that logical positivists are chiefly interested in logical and epistemological problems.

According to Victor Kraft, one of the members of the Vienna Circle, besides agreement on general features of logical positivism different members expressed different views on various issues. Kraft writes:

> The composition of the Vienna Circle made it inevitable that there would be no such uniformity of views as might be expected in a mere circle of disciples who simply adopt teacher's opinion. For, after all, at least the leading members were independent thinkers.[7]

This is the reason why we cannot give a comprehensive account of logical positivism since it involves a lot of patience and labour to explain each thinker's viewpoint on a certain issue. The members of the Circle claim to differ in their formulations of theories such as principle of verification, probability, etc. For example, Schlick demanded conclusive verification, whereas

---

6. Victor Kraft, *The Vienna Circle* (New York, 1969), p. 26.
7. Ibid., p. 15.

Ayer and others suggested verifiability in its stronger and weaker senses as it would be impossible to verify a statement conclusively. Carnap suggested confirmability in the place of verifiability. But whatever the differences they have with regard to their approach, their priorities are the same. In spite of their subtle differences, the common claim acceptable to all the members of the Circle is that they regard language as the only subject matter of philosophy and its method is analysis. Even the types of analysis differ from thinker to thinker. Schlick and his followers were more interested in semantic analysis whereas Carnap showed some negative attitude towards semantics and concentrated more on syntax.

Logical positivists' campaign against metaphysics and to eliminate it from philosophy has had both positive and negative aspects. The positive aspect of their campaign is that traditional speculative philosophy showed very little interest in concrete problems of human life and scientific cognition. In other words, it laid too much emphasis on idealism and religion. The negative aspect of their campaign is that they rejected all the traditional problems of philosophy as they are unrelated to science. Instead of giving a new scientific impetus to these problems, they (logical positivists) discarded all the fundamental problems of philosophy as metaphysical. They include the problems concerning objectivity, necessity, causation, essence, etc. Such problems, according to logical positivists, are beyond the purview of sense-experience. Consequently, they do not comply with the basic tenets of logical positivism. For logical positivists, scientific knowledge is the knowledge of the objects of sensation which is confined to the appearances of the objects. Like Berkeley and Hume, logical positivists too abolished the distinction between appearance and reality. They consider that every appearance is real. In fact, the legacy of Hume is well maintained by logical positivists by giving a new colour to it. However, the negative attitude towards metaphysics is so strong that they made it a characteristic feature of their thought. To quote Schlick's remarks in this context:

> If one wishes to characterise every view which denies the possibility of metaphysics as positivistic, this is quite unobjectionable as a mere definition, and I should in this sense call myself a strict positivist.[8]

The positivist flavour is shown in the above statement of Moritz Schlick. Scientific temper is an essential prerequisite for any positivist.

In an attempt to overcome metaphysics (speculative thinking), logical positivists put forward a detailed programme through which they can provide a logical structure of the entire edifice of science with a view to standardising the language of science. They have also indulged in identifying the basic elements of knowledge (sense-data) and reducing entire science to those elements. Apart from that, logical positivists fully made use of mathematical logic of Russell as an agency through which they could accomplish their new tasks. Nevertheless, all the attempts of logical positivists were in vain for obvious reasons. The basic premises of logical positivism are not sound enough to protect their interests.

Logical positivists conceive that all the philosophical problems arise out of misunderstanding of the meaning of statements in everyday language and science. They consider that analysis is used as a method to bring out the "logical implications" of concepts and propositions of everyday language and science. They maintain that the propositions of philosophy are not factual, but linguistic in their character. According to F. Waismann:

> The analytical method leads us to the view that the questions themselves rest upon misunderstanding; it frees us from them

8. Moritz Schlick, "Positivism and Realism", in A.J. Ayer (ed.), *Logical Positivism* (London, 1960), p. 83.

> by making the meaning of our words clear and the way they are combined in language so clear that we no longer feel driven to ask questions.[9]

Similar view is expressed by A.J. Ayer, the leading British exponent of logical positivism. Trying to clarify the stand of logical positivists Ayer holds that the function of philosophy is philosophical analysis. The following quotation of Ayer suggests to us the most useful function of the philosopher.

> But where in that case does the philosopher come in? One thing he can do, of course, is to act as a sort of intellectual policeman, seeing that nobody trespasses into metaphysics. In the *Tractatus*, Wittgenstein seemed to think that this was all that he can do. . . . The Vienna Circle, however, was not content with quite so negative a conception of philosophy as this. They thought that the philosopher still had a useful function to perform, in analysing and clarifying the concepts which figure in the everyday, and also in the scientific, use of language, but chiefly in the scientific use, as this was held to be the more important. Philosophy was to become the logic of science. In a sense, philosophy was to merge with science. There would not be a set of philosophical statements embedded among the scientific ones, but the scientific statements themselves would be refined by logical analysis.[10]

This quotation of A.J. Ayer brings out the true spirit of logical positivism. Unlike Wittgenstein, logical positivists were not contented with the role of philosopher as an "intellectual policeman" to prevent people from indulging in speculative thinking, but assigned a new job to philosopher. The new job of philosopher was to clarify the concepts of everyday language and science. Thus philosophy, for logical positivists, becomes

---

9. F. Waismann, *The Principles of Linguistic Philosophy* (London, 1968), p. 5.
10. A.J. Ayer, "Vienna Circle", in his *The Revolution in Philosophy*, pp. 78-79.

a logic of science. This does not mean that propositions of philosophy consist of scientific element in them. Victor Kraft holds: "Philosophy is not a science with a subject matter of its own, but a method which is employed in the special sciences whenever and wherever there occur obscurities."[11] Philosophy, thus, is regarded as a method rather than a discipline with a definite subject matter. Such method is identified with analysis.

The downfall of logical positivism is largely attributed to be internal contradictions that are prevalent in its own structure and also its inadequacy in understanding the genuine nature of the scientific investigation. We shall not focus our attention on the issues that preoccupied logical positivism at different stages of its evolution. Some of the important features of the logical positivism have been taken into account for a detailed study. Our contention in this study would be to show that the doctrines of logical positivism rest upon the premises which are objectively false. In addition, the theories advocated by logical positivists are in glaring contradiction to actual scientific proof. It is aptly pointed out by Feuer that logical positivism's

> . . . distinctive doctrines are not the products of a dispassionate analysis of scientific practice. They are rather expression of a group of scholars . . . by interposing extraneous components of science within scientific statements.[12]

In spite of their repeated claims that their (logical positivists') philosophy differs from the traditional empiricism, in the final analysis, logical positivism is in no way different from the traditional empiricism of Berkeley and Hume.

As pointed out earlier, it is very difficult to give a comprehensive picture of logical positivism because of the

---

11. Victor Kraft, *The Vienna Circle*, p. 188.
12. Lewis S. Feuer, "The Development of Logical Empiricism", *Science and Society*, New York, vol. V, 1941, p. 222.

diversity of opinions offered by the individual thinkers on various aspects. Keeping this in view, our main emphasis in this study would be on A.J. Ayer's version of logical positivism. Now we shall confine ourselves to the doctrines of Ayer and attempt to examine the aspects related to the method and the subject matter of philosophy, principle of verification as the criterion of meaning, causality and problem of induction, sense-data as the ultimate constituents of reality, knowledge of other minds and statements about the past.

3

The Nature and Method of Philosophy

LIKE any other logical positivist, Ayer maintains that the sole function of philosophy is the logical analysis of language. Accordingly, he conceives that the subject matter of philosophy is language and its professed method is analysis. One wonders as to what made logical positivists to assign this peculiar function to philosophy. They (logical positivists) believe that every science has its own subject matter to deal with. For example, zoology deals with animal kingdom, botany with plant kingdom, physics with the physical properties of the objects, astronomy with celestial bodies, etc. In this way, there is nothing specific left to philosophy to project. Claiming to save philosophy from this rather awkward situation, logical positivists assigned philosophy the function of logical analysis of language. Ayer holds that philosopher does not indulge in any kind of experimentation; he does not patiently observe the behaviour of any natural objects, yet philosophy purports to provide us with a definite "knowledge" which is different from that of scientific one. Then the question before logical positivists is: What kind of knowledge does philosophical activity result in? To put it simply — what then is philosophical analysis?

Nature of Philosophical Analysis

Analysis is a process in which composites are divided into various samples. This activity is quite common in sciences. For instance, physicists analyse matter into atoms and these atoms are further analysed into sub-atomic particles like electrons, protons, neutrons, neutrinos, quarks, etc. This type of analysis is chiefly practised in science in order to know the inner structure of various elements. But what kind of analysis does a philosopher do? As expressed by Ayer, there are no elements in philosophy to conduct experiments on them. Moreover, it is not the business of a philosopher to detect the behaviour of natural phenomena. In an attempt to answer this question, Ayer makes it clear that philosophical analysis is concerned with the use and function of language. This analysis consists in rewriting sentences of everyday language and science in such a way that these sentences will exhibit their proper logical form. When they are put into their proper logical form, their meaning will become clear and philosophical perplexities will be cleared. As a result of this approach, maintains Ayer, the traditional problems of philosophy are found to disappear. Like Wittgenstein of *Tractatus*, Ayer opines that the problems of philosophy appear due to muddled thinking, but this muddled thinking itself is largely the product of lack of accurate use of language. The analysis practised by Wittgenstein in his *Tractatus* can be called "world analysis," whereas the analysis practised by Ayer is "word analysis." In what follows we shall attempt to show that Ayer misinterprets the function of philosophy by reducing it to mere logical analysis of language. This function of philosophy does not yield any knowledge of reality. In other words, Ayer's notion of philosophy deprives philosophy of any epistemological content. Apart from that, Ayer takes it for granted as if language were a ready-made thing without taking its development into consideration. Let us examine Ayer's views on the nature and method of philosophy in detail.

In defence of his view, namely, the function of philosophy is analysis of language, Ayer argues that philosophy is not a search for "first principles." As a matter of fact, Ayer's attack is indirectly directed against Aristotle and René Descartes. The celebrated Greek philosopher and scientist, Aristole envisaged that "metaphysics" is the first philosophy. It always aims at finding the specific causes of philosophy. These first principles, according to Aristotle, lead us to certain knowledge of reality. Similarly, René Descartes (1596-1650) arrived at his first principle of philosophy *cogito ergo sum* (I think, therefore I am) with his doubting method in order to construct a profound and consistent system of philosophy. Ayer holds the view:

> . . . the function of these first principles is to provide a certain basis for our knowledge, it is clear that they are not to be found among the so-called laws of nature. For we shall see that the "laws are nature," if they are not mere definitions, are simply hypotheses which may be confuted by experience.[1]

Ayer believes that the "first principles" are not deduced from an intuitively perceived truth upon which a philosopher proceeds to construct a deductive system. They are, argues Ayer, no objects of speculative knowledge which lies beyond empirical investigation. Ayer maintains that if at all anyone wants to deduce all our knowledge from "first principles" without making any inroads into "metaphysics" he must take a priori truth as his premises. But, asserts Ayer, all the a priori truths are tautologies. From a set of tautologies we can deduce another set of tautologies, but not empirical truths.[2] Thus, Ayer claims to arrive at the view that it is not possible to deduce all our knowledge from the "first principles." What then, according to Ayer, does the activity of philosophising consist of?

According to Ayer, the activity of philosophising is essentially analytic. He says that "all those who are commonly called philosophers have actually been engaged in carrying out

1. A.J. Ayer, *Language, Truth and Logic*, p. 62.
2. Ibid., p. 63.

analysis."[3] This statement of Ayer suggests to us that to be a philosopher one has to be an analyst. Not only that, "it can be shown that the majority of those who are commonly supposed to have been great philosophers were primarily not metaphysicians but analysts."[4] This statement of Ayer is quite misleading, because the history of philosophy reveals us that the philosophers like Plato, Aristotle, Descartes, Kant, Hegel and Marx contributed so much for the development of philosophy. They have been rated as most original and influential thinkers of their respective times. In spite of the fact that Plato's philosophy involves lots of metaphysics, Plato has been regarded as one of the greatest Greek thinkers, who provided us with a comprehensive account of reality. Similarly, Aristotle's entire philosophy is centred around his "metaphysics." Therefore, it is a folly to think that metaphysicians do not involve in any kind of analysis. A thinker cannot propound his theory without giving a proper analysis of it. It is true that Plato used metaphors and analysis to illustrate his theories about metaphysics and its relation to social construction. No one rules out this fact. Plato used analysis as a mere tool, but not as an end product of his philosophy. Ayer goes on to argue that all his empiricist pioneers (Locke, Berkeley and Hume) are great because they were involved in the activity of analysis. To quote Ayer's remarks on these philosophers:

> Locke is generally regarded as being one who . . . puts forward a philosophy of common sense. But he does not, anymore than Moore, attempt to give an a priori justification of our common sense beliefs. Rather does he appear to have seen that it was not his business as a philosopher to affirm or deny the validity of any empirical propositions, but only to analyse them. . . . Nor is it fair to regard Berkeley as a

3. A.J. Ayer, *Language, Truth and Logic*, p. 69.

4. Ibid., p. 70.

> metaphysician. For he did not, in fact, deny the reality of material things, as we are still too commonly told.[5]

Let us then suppose that Locke and Berkeley have merely analysed the contents of our sense-experiences not to prove or disprove anything, but to know how effective the activity of analysis would be. In that case, whatever they advocated should be taken not in a true sense, but only in a pejorative sense. The disastrous consequence of such a view is that analysts are not to be taken very seriously. As a matter of fact, the same conception of Berkeley towards the existence of material objects has been adopted by Ayer. On the pretext of "analysing" the concepts of everyday language and science, Ayer reduces the statements about material objects to statements about sense-data. The purpose of reductionist thesis is to deny the existence of material objects. This aspect will be elaborated in due course while discussing Ayer's theory of perception.

Regarding Hume's analysis, Ayer holds that Hume is opposed to metaphysics. Ayer writes as follows:

> Of Hume we may say that merely he was not in practice a metaphysician, but that he explicitly rejected metaphysics. . . . It is true that Hume does not, so far as I know, actually put forward any view concerning the nature of philosophical propositions themselves, but those of his works which are commonly accounted philosophical are . . . works of analysis. If this is not universally conceded, it is because his treatment of causation, which . . . is often misinterpreted.[6]

In support of Hume, Ayer says that he too is opposed to metaphysics. Hume rejected the metaphysics of transcendental kind on the ground that the statements of metaphysics are neither derived through relations of ideas nor through matters

---

5. A.J. Ayer, *Language, Truth and Logic*, p. 69
6. Ibid., p. 72.

of fact. But Hume has provided us with some analysis in showing that metaphysical statements are non-sensical. In similar fashion, he rejected the necessary causal connection between events in reality. If what Hume said about metaphysics should be taken seriously, then his views on causation should also be taken seriously, because both the views are products of the same analysis. Ayer himself subscribes to the Humean conception of causation. We shall discuss this point in detail while discussing Ayer's views on causation and induction. Ayer claims that the activity of analysis is the characteristic feature of British empiricism.

Having satisfied with his conviction that all the great philosophers in the past were basically analysts, Ayer puts forward the following views with regard to the analysis practised by philosophers in general. To quote Ayer's views in this context:

> For the philosopher, as an analyst, is not directly concerned with the physical properties of things. He is concerned only with the way in which we speak about them. In other words, the propositions of philosophy are not factual, but linguistic in character, that is, they do not describe the behaviour of physical or even mental objects; they express definitions, or the formal consequences of definitions . . . the possibility of philosophical analysis is independent of any empirical assumptions. . . .[7]

What follows from the above quotation of Ayer is that the philosopher as an analyst is more concerned about the language that we use in describing the nature of the things. Therefore, the statements of the philosopher are not to be taken as factual information about the nature of the things. What, then, is the status of the statements of a philosopher? The statements of a philosopher are mere linguistic expressions about an object or

7. A.J. Ayer, *Language, Truth and Logic*, p. 76.

thing in question. For example, ". . . to ask what is the nature of a material object is to ask for a definition of a material object. . . ."[8] A philosopher, then, is different from all other human beings. He can define anything according to his whims and fancies without taking facts into consideration. The language used by a philosopher is understood only by another philosopher with similar tastes. According to Ayer, a philosopher does not, or should not, as he has been commonly understood to do, analyse "facts" or notions or even "things."[9] It is only in a Pickwikian sense, i.e. regardless of their actual or literal sense, that "facts" or "notions" or "things" can be said to exist to be analysed. In this way, Ayer, a professed empiricist, discarded all empirical facts, for they are irrelevant to philosophy. For he considers that a philosopher should be concerned only with the stipulative definitions of his own inventions. This is clear from the following statement of Ayer:

> It may be suggested, therefore, that if I wish to give a strict account of my present visual experience, I must make a more cautious statement. I must say not that I see the cigarette case, if this is to carry the implication that there is a cigarette case there, but only that it seems to me that I am seeing it . . . The next step continuing with our example is to convert the sentence "it now seems to me that I see a cigarette case" into I am now seeing a seeming cigarette case. And this seeming cigarette case, which lives only in my present experience, is an example of a sense-datum.[10]

In the fantasy world of a philosopher everything appears to be a shade of the original. The philosopher is more concerned about how shades look like than the originals. The existence of

---

8. A.J. Ayer, *Language, Truth and Logic*, p. 78.
9. Ibid., p. 79
10. A.J. Ayer, *The Problem of Knowledge* (Harmondsworth, 1977), p. 96.

the original is something that does not concern him. Every shade is identified with a sense-datum. It is the sense-datum which is important for the philosopher to carry out his activity of analysis.

Ayer distinguishes science from philosophy. Science, asserts Ayer, is the systematic knowledge of the reality, and "there is not, there cannot be, a philosophical brand of knowledge which would compete with science in this field."[11] Moreover, opines Ayer, the distinction between philosophy and science or any other subject is made not on the basis of former's subject matter but by its methods. The arguments, according to Ayer, used by philosophers have some peculiar character. Philosophical proofs, unlike in mathematics, do not consist of formal demonstrations. They are also not tested by observation. The theories of philosophy are neutral with regard to particular matters of fact.[12] This view of Ayer drives us to the conclusion that all philosophical formulations are deprived of empirical content. They are mere mumblings of the philosophers without any seriousness.

The statement that all the formulations of philosophy are of different kinds needs a clarification. In what way the formulations of philosophers are different from those of scientists? In an attempt to clarify this point, Ayer holds that the questions such as whether the material objects are real, whether objects continue to exist at times when they are not perceived cannot be decided on the basis of scientific information. They are not, believes Ayer, the questions which could be settled by conducting experiments but can be resolved on the basis of analysis of language. To quote Ayer in this context:

---

11. A.J. Ayer, "The Vienna Circle", in his *The Revolution in Philosophy*, p. 78.
12. A.J. Ayer, *The Problem of Knowledge*, p. 7.

> What is in dispute in such cases is not whether, in a given set of circumstances, this or that event will happen, but rather how anything at all that happens is to be described.[13]

How could anything in question be described without taking its factual content into account? If one does so, then it is not the description of anything in question. The analytical activity undertaken by Ayer appears to be strange. What exactly does this activity of philosophical analysis consist of? According to Ayer, philosophical analysis consists of providing definitions.

Definitions in Use

Ayer, in defence of his position, argues that the definitions provided by philosophy are not "explicit definitions" but "definitions in use." Trying to bring out the distinction between the definitions of lexicographer and the definitions of philosopher, Ayer writes:

> . . . a lexicographer also seeks to give information about the usage of words, but the philosophers differ from him in being concerned . . . not with the use of particular expressions but with classes of expressions; and whereas the propositions of the lexicographer are empirical, philosophical propositions, if they are true, are usually analytic.[14]

A lexicographer, in the view of Ayer, is an empirical scientist, who glosses the terms according to their usage. Therefore, his definitions have an empirical content. But the definitions of philosophers, says Ayer, are analytic in their nature. Ayer supposes that the definitions in use show, "how the sentences in which if a symbol significantly occurs can be translated into equivalent sentences, which contain neither the definition itself, nor any of its synonyms."[15] Thus Ayer argues that every

13. A.J. Ayer, *The Problem of Knowledge*, p. 7

14. A.J. Ayer, *Language, Truth and Logic*, p. 34.

15. Ibid., p. 81.

sentence which consists of a symbolic expression can be translated into a sentence which does not contain any such expression, but does contain a sub-sentence asserting that one and only one object possesses a certain property, or else that no one subject possesses a certain property.[16] To exemplify, the sentence that "the round square does not exist," is equivalent to "No one thing can be both round and square," and the sentence that "The author of *Waverley* was Scotch" is equivalent to "one person, and one person only, wrote *Waverley*, and that person was Scotch."[17] This analysis of Ayer reveals that a sentence of an equivalence is, if correct, a tautology; if incorrect, a contradiction.

Susan Stebbing in her review article on Ayer's *Language, Truth and Logic*, points out that the statement "The author of *Waverley* was Scotch" is translated into an equivalent statement that "One person and one person only wrote *Waverley* and that person was Scotch," results in violation of the rules of analysis set forth by Ayer. Stebbing argues that if the word "that" is used referentially, then "that person was Scotch" is equivalent to the whole of the original; and if it is used demonstratively, the defining expression is not a translation of the original at all.[18] In an attempt to defend his position, Ayer remarks:

> . . . the object of analysing "The author of *Waverley* was Scotch" is not just to obtain an accurate translation of this particular sentence, but to elucidate the use of a whole class of expressions, of which "the author of *Waverley*" serves merely as a typical example.[19]

16. A.J. Ayer, *Language, Truth and Logic*, pp. 111-82.
17. To explain the nature of analytical activity, Ayer takes these examples from Russell's theory of descriptions and the illustrations contained are also those of Russell's.
18. L.S. Stebbing, "Ayer's Language, Truth and Logic", *Mind* (London), N.S., vol. XLV, no. 45, 1936, p. 358.
19. A.J. Ayer, *Language, Truth and Logic*, p. 31.

Ayer claims that this example is given to show how certain class of expressions can be explained in our ordinary language. Accordingly, believes Ayer, if a philosopher sticks to such analysis he will avoid either interfering in the sphere of natural science or involving himself in metaphysics. But one does not understand as to why a philosopher should not indulge in the analysis of statements of metaphysics. If the statements of philosophers do not have any empirical content, then statements of metaphysics also do not have any empirical content. Then, in what way are the statements of philosophy superior to those of metaphysics? This needs to be clarified.

Proceeding further, Ayer tries to define an ambiguous symbol that occurs in a statement. He writes:

> . . . that a symbol is constituted by signs which are identical with one another in their sensible form, and in their significance, and that sign is a sense content, or a series of sense contents, which is used to convey literal meaning, is not to say that a symbol is a collection or system of sense contents.[20]

From the above statement of Ayer we can infer that he is heading for reductive analysis. It shows that a "symbol" is reducible to "signs" which are identical in their sensible form. For example, "material object" is an ambiguous symbol. It can be reduced to a series of "sense contents" which are signs of that symbol? The problem one confronts here is, how can one define an ambiguous symbol? Ambiguities cannot be reduced into signs. Then those signs will also be ambiguous, if the symbol and its signs are identical in their sensible form. Ayer's fancy for reductive analysis is seen in the following quotation:

> We may explain the nature of logical constructions by saying that the introduction of symbols which denote logical

20. A.J. Ayer, *Language, Truth and Logic*, p. 84.

> constructions is a device which enables us to state complicated propositions about the elements of these constructions in relatively simple form.[21]

For he considers that the propositions about material objects are complicated and can be translated into propositions about sense contents or sense-data which are supposed to be simpler units of our experience. Ayer presupposes:

> The problem of giving an actual rule for translating sentences about a material thing into sentences about sense contents, which may be called the problem of the "reduction" of material things to sense contents is the main philosophical part of the traditional problem of perception.[22]

Although the problem of perception is regarded as one of the important problems in the history of philosophy, none other than twentieth-century analysts ever tried to reduce material objects to something else. The philosophers of the past like Plato, Descartes and other rationalists rejected sensory knowledge as erroneous or accepted it partially. However, they never suspected the very existence of material world.

Justifying the reasons for adopting this reductive analysis, Ayer states:

> . . . that certain types of entity are philosophically suspect, and the purpose is to show that references to such entities are nevertheless innocuous; They can be construed as disguised references to entities which are relatively less problematic.[23]

It implies that the propositions expressing facts of ordinary perceptual knowledge contain such expressions like "table" and

---

21. A.J. Ayer, *Language, Truth and Logic,* p. 85
22. Ibid., p. 86.
23. A.J. Ayer, "Philosophy and Language", in his *Concept of a Person and Other Essays* (London, 1973), p. 13.

"chairs," but such objects and their properties and relations are not simple, and so are not the ultimate constituents of our sensory knowledge. This is precisely what Ayer means by "some entities are problematic." And when the propositions containing such expressions are analysed, they will be expressed in terms of ultimate constituents. In other words, ordinary unanalysed knowledge seems to be about such things as "tables," "chairs," etc. but analysis will make it clear the ultimate constituents of the knowledge. Thus Ayer identifies philosophy with analysis and emphasises "that the only positive contribution that philosophy can make to knowledge is in the field of analysis."[24]

From the above account of Ayer's views on philosophical analysis, one realises that logical positivists are maintaining the heritage of their empiricist predecessors by upholding Berkelian analysis of "physical objects" and Humean analysis of "causation." The business is still the old reductive analysis (phenomenalism) even under the new management.

The chief aim of Ayer and all other logical positivists in identifying philosophy with analysis is to dismiss all those aspects related to objective material world as irrelevant. If all that a philosopher can do is the logical analysis of concepts of everyday language and science, then what kind of knowledge do we acquire about the objective reality? Thus the analysis of Ayer takes us away from the path of knowledge into the path of empty arguments about words or concepts.

Critical Reflections

Some main objections come from Max Black, John Wisdom, Gilbert Ryle, Maurice Cornforth and G.J. Warnock against this kind of "analysis." This does not mean that they are not in

24. A.J. Ayer, "Philosophy and Science", in his *Metaphysics and Common Sense* (London, 1973), p. 82.

favour of analysis as a method in philosophy, but interpret analysis in an altogether different way.

Max Black stresses on the view that analysis is a useful method in philosophy. He considers that analysis is a method of ostentation. His views are based on the firm conviction that analysis is the analysis of facts, but not of the meaning of statements. For instance, the facts such as "Mr Jones sat down," "Mr Jones is in his study," etc. can be pointed out. According to Black, every true proposition represents a fact. This is what Black means by "ostentation." In the absence of any representation our analysis of words, sentences, and statements would be a futile exercise. With a view to differentiating "philosophical analysis" from "logical analysis," Black observes:

> . . . that the analytic method under consideration is either considered with the analysis of facts in the sense of fact in which the same fact corresponds to different sentences, or, if it is regarded as concerned with analysing the meaning of statements or sentences, analyse those statements into conjunctions of statements entailed by, but not having the same meaning as, the analysandum. It is this fact which distinguishes ostentation or philosophical analysis from logical analysis; which is concerned with the expression of statements into statements of identical meaning.[25]

Black's interest appears to be more in factual analysis (world analysis) rather than in mere sentential analysis. He shares with logical atomists in identifying philosophical analysis with factual analysis in order to show that there is a one-to-one correspondence between language and reality. Even Russell stressed on ostentation. Black feels that logical analysis is more semantic-oriented. Thus he claims that the analysis practised

---

25. Max Black, "Is Analysis a Useful Method in Philosophy?", *Proceedings of the Aristotelian Society Supplement* (London), vol. 13, no. 13, 1934, p. 55.

by him is different from the logical analysis of the Vienna Circle.

Like Max Black, John Wisdom too holds the view that analysis is an old and very useful method in philosophy. But, unlike Max Black, Wisdom identifies philosophical analysis with linguistic analysis. For he believes that philosophical analysis is something different from material analysis. Wisdom, while clarifying the distinction between philosophical and material analyses, illustrates:

> Whenever one analyses the fact that S is P, one gives an ostensive translation of the sentence "S" is "P" . . . this is because to do the one is to do the other with a certain intention. It does not follow that to analyse the fact, the economic man always buys in the best market is to analyse the sentence, "the economic man always buys in the best market." To suppose that it does follow is to fail to recognise the distinction between saying that analysis is a translation and saying that is a logical construction out of, i.e. may be philosophically analysed, into, translation. It is nonsense to talk of analysing sentences.[26]

Wisdom appears to be more scrupulous in his approach. According to him, philosophical analysis is nothing but logical analysis, namely, analysis of language. Like Black, Wisdom stresses on the ostensive translation of the sentences. Every ostensive translation, says Wisdom, results in material analysis. We normally analyse facts, but not the sentences. Our analysis of facts takes sentential form. This does not mean that we engage ourselves in analysing the sentences without bothering about the facts that they depict. The confusion that arises, opines Wisdom, between the analysis as a translation of the fact into a sentence and analysis as a translation of the facts

26. John Wisdom, "Is Analysis a Useful Method in Philosophy?", *Proceedings of the Aristotelian Society Supplement*, vol. 13, no. 13, 1934, p. 65.

into logical constructs is unwarranted. Thus he is very critical about reductive analysis.

In order to throw some more light on this confusion, Wisdom argues that a scientist gives a material analysis of the object of his investigation. Similarly, an economist gives a material analysis of wealth, if he defines it what is useful, transferable and limited in supply. Wisdom contends that "to give a material analysis is to give an analytic definition."[27] To exemplify, when a psychologist says that "I am in awe of you" meaning that "I fear and admire you," he is giving a material analysis of the fact those sentences express by giving more ostentation. For he thinks that the rules for translating sentences about the "biological rabbit," the "psychological individual" and "economic man" into sentences about rabbits and men give philosophical analysis.[28] This kind of analysis, says Wisdom, is meaningless. Therefore, actual analysis should be identified with material analysis.

Gilbert Ryle, in line with his ordinary language philosophy, puts forward the view that there are several types of expression which he considers to be systematically misleading. They are: quasi-ontological statements such as "Mr Baldwin is objective," "Mr Pickwick is subjective," quasi-Platonic statements like "Colour involves extension," quasi-descriptions which do not exhibit the real form of the fact in a way in which the form will be duly exhibited. But a new point of analysis is suggested, i.e. our purpose is no longer the ontological one of getting a clear view of the structure of reality, but to clear up linguistic puzzles and to prevent misconceptions about language and expose absurd theories. For instance, the sentence "Mr Baldwin is a politician" exhibits the form of the fact. It is not in need of any analysis, hence it is not misleading. But the sentence "Mr

27. John Wisdom, op. cit., p. 66.

28. Ibid.

Baldwin is subjective" does not exhibit the form of the fact. It needs to be analysed. Otherwise it is misleading. Though there is an obscure reference to the form of fact in such sentences, says Ryle, it is like a vestigial human appendix without any function.[29] Ryle arrives at the following conclusion:

> . . . that there is, after all, a sense in which we can properly enquire and even say "what it really means to say so and so." For we can ask what is the real form of the fact recorded when it is concealed or disguised and not duly exhibited by the expression in question. And we can often succeed in stating this fact in a new form of words which does exhibit what the other failed to exhibit. And I am for the present inclined to believe that this is the sole and whole function of philosophy.[30]

Prior to Ryle, it was Russell who insisted on the analysis of misleading statements like "The present king of France is bald." He felt that the grammatical form of the sentence does not reveal its logical form. In order to expose its logical form Russell introduced his famous theory of descriptions. But there is a difference in approach between Russell and Ryle to solve the philosophical puzzlements. Russell's analysis is ontological, whereas the analysis of Ryle is purely linguistic. Moreover, Russell's main objective is to protect the law of excluded middle. According to this law, a genuine proposition is one that it must be either true or false.

G.J. Warnock, an Oxford philosopher with a considerable reputation, feels that the analysis practised by the contemporary analytic philosophers cannot completely overcome philosophical riddles. The aim of analysis, according to these philosophers, is to remove unclarity of words and

---

29. Gilben Ryle, "Systematically Misleading Expressions", in his *Collected Essays* (London, 1971), p. 60.

30. Ibid., p. 61.

expressions that we use in language. This results in, opines Warnock, finding out certain more "explicit" but less "concentrated" use of words which will be logically equivalent to that which is analysed. But, argues Warnock, our language does not contain such locutions. Even if it contains, we can classify, by means of this analysis, only the entailments, the narrowly defined logical features of puzzling expressions, but not all the problems concerning the langauge. To quote Warnock in this context:

> To confine oneself to the pursuit of . . . analyses is in effect to concentrate upon, at best only a small part of the use of our words and expressions; but the cause of our troubles may lie in our imperfect grasp of any feature of that use; there is, accordingly, no guarantee whatever that an analysis, even if it could be convincingly formulated, would alleviate our philosophical troubles. The most serious objection, then, to the programme of analysis is not that it is doubtful how far such analyses can be produced — though this is, in fact, quite a serious objection — it is rather that, even if they could be produced, they may well be philosophically unprofitable.[31]

There is some meaning in Warnock's arguments. After all, what for this ceremony called analysis is performed? As rightly pointed out by Warnock, this kind of analysis disarms the very spirit of philosophy and reduces philosophy to a barren field.

Castigating the method of analysis practised in philosophy, Maurice Cornforth rightly observes how far this method of analysis is useful in the acquisition of knowledge of reality. He poses a question that if philosophical analysis is not a means of advancing our knowledge, then in the sense intended in the question, it is not a useful method in philosophy.[32] In line with

31. G.I. Warnock, *English Philosophy Since 1900* (London, 1969), p. 86.

32. Maurice Cornforth, "Is Analysis a Useful Method in Philosophy?", *Proceedings of the Aristotelian Society Supplement*, vol. 13, no. 13, 1934, p. 90.

his dialectical materialist[33] approach, Cornforth argues against the method of analysis. According to him, the method of analysis adopted by recent analytic philosophers explains that the "elements" of facts displayed in a new level of analysis are "more ultimate than those which were displayed before the analysis took place."[34] This is to say that the ordinary products of our common sense and scientific knowledge are not clear as to the ultimate character of the facts to which they refer. It is necessary to undertake a fresh process of investigation, a process of the philosophical analysis of those results, in order to find out what it is to which ultimately it refers. Cornforth contests that this interpretation then seeks to show that the ultimate elements to which our scientific and common sense knowledge refer are sensations or sense data. It seeks to show that such knowledge is really and ultimately concerned with the order of occurrences in human experience. Consequently, the whole tendency of philosophical analysis is in direction of phenomenalism and concludes that "analytic philosophy is just as speculative as speculative philosophy."[35] Moreover, the analysis presented by logical positivists (modern empiricists) is in a logical light. What is stressed in the logical distinction between propositions at different levels is the proposition to be analysed and its analysis. What is not taken care of is the epistemological distinction between discovery and analysis. Cornforth emphasises: "The discovery is the work of science or common sense; the analysis of that is the work of philosophy."[36] What Cornforth intends to say is that the business of science is to deal with the reality and to discover the things

33. Regarding his approach, Cornforth makes it very clear in the above-mentioned article that his method is dialectical materialist method, which studies things and phenomena in their inter-connections.

34. Ibid., p. 95.

35. Ibid., p. 98.

36. Ibid.

in their inter-relatedness. On the contrary, the business of a philosopher is to interpret them. This is precisely what Cornforth means by analysis here.

Like John Wisdom, Cornforth is also critical of reductive analysis. The phenomenalistic interpretation of material objects, holds Cornforth, is "a misinterpretation of character of knowledge."[37] The main aim of such analysis is to distort the whole picture of reality by merely concentrating on the logic of langauge as if language were a ready-made thing. The philosophy as a method ". . . is to unravel the general laws of motion of all real processes, to elucidate the general principles of all real changes and developments and to explain by what means men are able to gain accurate knowledge of the world in which they live."[38]

The above account of Cornforth has clearly brought out the distinction between scientific and pseudo-scientific philosophy of logical positivism. For the purpose of further clarification and comparison, we shall state philosophical foundations and real subject matter of philosophy and its relation to scientific world view. This would help us to expose the setbacks of Ayer's conception of philosophy and its method. In fact, the charges that are going to be levelled against Ayer are equally applicable to all those who profess that subject matter of philosophy is language and its legitimate method is analysis.

Philosophy as Synthesis

Philosophy is a synthetic unity of various forms and levels of human experiences. It deals with the most general account of Nature and our place in it. This is all the more important because philosophers are not unanimous on this point. As we have seen,

37. Maurice Cornforth, op. cit., p. 102.

38. Ibid., p. 118.

Ayer and other logical positivists are under the impression that there is no integral philosophical system that is embraced by one and all. A philosopher creates his own system. They believe that philosophy occupies an intermediatory position between science and metaphysics (theology).[39] According to Ayer, all definite knowledge belongs to science and all dogma that supersedes definite knowledge belongs to metaphysics. Between science and metaphysics, logical positivists believe there is a third line exposed to attack from both the sides. This third line is philosophy. It is evident from Ayer's account that the introduction of analysis as a method is to prevent the philosopher from trespassing into science and metaphysics. Therefore, philosophy can survive as an independent branch of knowledge. This attitude of Ayer towards philosophy is one sided or even erroneous in the context of modern scientific conception of philosophy. For instance, philosophy differs from art. Art serves to satisfy people's aesthetic requirements and reflects reality in the form of artistic images; whereas philosophy has always purported to satisfy man's requirements in explaining the nature of the world, which is done through the abstract notions, categories and laws. Nor can we identify philosophy with religion. Religion is a reflection of natural and social reality of those external forces that dominate men in their everyday life. In religious consciousness the world and being are interpreted through a belief in supernatural entities. Religion is, therefore, opposed to science as a system of objectively true knowledge of the reality in which men are a part. Unlike religion, philosophy operates with theoretical abstractions[40] rather than illusory images. It does not rely on

39. For logical positivists, science deals with the order of sensations or sense contents, while "metaphysics" deals with supersensible reality. This point has been discussed in the subsequent chapters.

40. The principles of philosophy are derived from the empirical world and are applicable back to that world. It is here that the validity of philosophical principles rests.

the postulated dogmas, but tries to explain being on the basis of knowledge of reality. In other words, the problems of philosophy are the problems of life.

Certainly, Ayer too claims to get rid of metaphysics from the sphere of philosophy to make philosophy a genuine branch of knowledge like any other logical positivist. However, Ayer's position results in abstractions[41] because of his confinement to a specific problem of analysis of language. This view of Ayer is also a form of metaphysics which regards things and phenomena as fixed and immutable. Like his world view, his conception of language is equally an abstract one. Language is a product of social activity of men. It is public and inter-subjective, and it is a means through which men express their views to fellow men. It has a specific and most important role to play in individuals' lives.

Ayer tries to distinguish science from philosophy on the ground that the former deals with the empirical facts whereas the latter deals with the stipulated definitions of its own. The theories of science can be tested by observation while the theories of philosophy cannot be. All the questions of philosophy, according to Ayer, can be resolved by mere analysis of language. In other words, the questions of philosophy are not of serious type. It is true that there is an essential difference between science and philosophy. The special sciences study the properties of various things, laws of Nature and society. Philosophy, on the other hand, is concerned with the general picture of the being, with a conception of the reality as a whole, in its multiformity and unity. The best illustration of the nature of science and philosophy is put forward by Henry Sidgwick. Scientific knowledge, asserts Sidgwick, is most systematic and grasped in a certain order. Its main aim is to establish a

---

41. They are mere abstractions which are purely speculative and have no links with the empirical world.

necessary causal relation between phenomena (facts). Above all, it is empirical and persuasive. With regard to philosophy, Sidgwick says:

> "Philosophy" then . . . as the study which "takes all knowledge for its province." To such a study the human mind would be palpably incompetent if it attempted to deal all the facts; it therefore selects the most important. Thus if we conceive the sciences as sets of connected knowledge, and imagine them rising from particular to general, we may consider these sets in their turn as connected by philosophy at the higher end. Philosophy, therefore, deals not with the whole matter of any science, but with the most important of its special notions, its fundamental principles, its distinctive method, its main conclusions. Philosophy examines these with the view of co-ordinating them with the fundamental notions and principles, methods and conclusions of other sciences. It may be called in this sense *scientia scientiarum*.[42]

The essential feature of philosophy is to arrange the knowledge of various sciences into a systematic whole with a view to presenting a harmonious, consistent and comprehensive account of the knowledge of the reality. Thus philosophy aims at understanding. Such an understanding of reality also involves critical approach towards fundamental beliefs of humans. As pointed out by C.D. Broad:

> It is obviously a necessary and a possible task, and it is not performed by any other science. The other sciences use the concepts and assume the beliefs; critical philosophy tries to analyse the former and to criticise the latter.[43]

A scientist wants to reveal the truth, while a philosopher does

42. Henry Sidgwick, "Philosophy as Synthesis", in Maurice Mandelbaum et al. (eds.) *Philosophic Problems* (New York, 1970), p. 6.
43. C.D. Broad, "Philosophy and Science", in Maurice Mandelbaum et al. (eds.), *Philosophic Problems*, p. 15.

not only strive to explain reality but also to interpret reality from the standpoint of science. Then the fundamental question of philosophy is to study the relation of consciousness to being because the answer to this question determines the solutions to all other problems, such as the unity of world, the essence of knowledge and ways of cognising the reality, etc. In fact, we have confined ourselves here to the task of philosophy in the acquisition of knowledge of the reality in contrast to Ayer's doctrine. We will discuss other aspects such as unity of world, the essence of knowledge, experience, etc. in the succeeding chapters.

The epitome of Ayer's doctrine is that philosophy is not a theory which explains reality in its interconnections but a kind of activity that analyses the concepts of everyday language and science. Ayer's philosophy has functional purpose, but no objective enquiry. This analysis of Ayer deprives philosophy of any cognitive activity of reality, confining merely to the subjective analysis of language.

4

The Principle of Verification

In the preceding chapter we have discussed the nature of the method of analysis and to what end it is practised in philosophy. The introduction of logical analysis as a method of philosophy, imagines Ayer, would prevent philosophers from indulging in the affairs of science as well as metaphysics. Not fully satisfied with their task, logical positivists attempted to draw a logical wedge between those statements that are verifiable, therefore "meaningful," and those statements that are not verifiable, therefore "meaningless." All those verifiable statements are supposed to have scientific character and all those unverifiable are supposed to be metaphysical in their nature. Here, the term "scientific" is being assumed that verification must always terminate in observation or sense-experience. For the sake of brevity and convenience this chapter has been divided into two sections. In the first section we shall confine ourselves to the principle of verification as a criterion of meaning in the context of supposed boundary between analytic and synthetic propositions resulting in the elimination of metaphysics of transcendental kind, and in the second section we will expound and examine the emotive theory of values.

I

What is Metaphysics?

Before initiating any discussion on the topic concerned it would be better to clarify what exactly one means by the term "metaphysics." A cursory look at the meaning of the term "metaphysics" would really help us in the present enquiry. The term "metaphysics" has different connotations in the history of philosophy. Traditionally, it is regarded that metaphysics deals with the essential and absolute nature of Reality as a whole or of the nature of being as such, i.e. the search for "first principles." The term "metaphysics" is derived from the Greek term *ta meta ta phusika*, which describes the first philosophy as a set of principles that come after physics. This originally means "what comes after physics" and generally referred to the works of Aristotle that followed his physics in the collection made by Andronicus. Aristotle defines metaphysics "as a science which investigates being as being and the attributes which belong to it in virtue of its own nature."[1] According to Aristotle, these first causes or principles need not exist in some world other than we live in but are very much part and parcel of this phenomenal world. Being a natural philosopher, his intentions in introducing the term "metaphysics" were something different as otherwise thought to be. His first philosophy is rather concerned with the causes of phenomena which could be unravelled by scientific investigation. Such causes, for Aristotle, constitute the essence of reality. There are large but finite number of things that for the most part belong to definite species, i.e. of plant and animal kingdoms. Eventually, however, the term "metaphysics" became popular in the history of philosophy as signifying that branch of philosophical enquiry which goes beyond physical events or substances.

The medieval and modern philosophers interpreted metaphysics in their own way. According to some interpretations, metaphysics deals with supersensible reality; to some it deals with the reality that transcends the limits of sensory observation; and to others it deals with the status of ultimate reality. In all these three cases, more than anything,

1. Aristotle, *Metaphysics* (London, 1956), Book 4, chapters I & II.

the term "reality" is in need of clarification. If one would like to interpret metaphysics as a doctrine that deals with super-sensible reality, then there are several scientific entities which are not comprehended by ordinary sense-perception. For example, none of the senses could provide us with any clue about the structure of atom, energy, time, consciousness, etc. They are only arrived at by means of thought experiments. In spite of their imperceptible nature these entities are very much part and parcel of this physical world. Physicists say that matter can be converted into energy, but energy is not seen or touched. We can only feel the manifestations of energy, though these scientific entities are imperceptible. They do not transcend the limits of empirical investigation,[2] yet they are metaphysical entities in one sense of the term. There is another set of entities which are neither perceptible nor empirically verifiable. They are the entities like *Brahman*, *Ātman*, Absolute Spirit, God, soul, etc. If one were to consider the view that metaphysics is concerned with the status of ultimate reality, then what science views as ultimately real can also be called metaphysical. Unless one makes it clear as to how one interprets the term metaphysics, it is very difficult to derive the exact meaning from it. Keeping all these difficulties in mind, we would like to interpret metaphysics as the science or doctrine that deals with the status of ultimate reality. It is immaterial whether reality is perceptible or imperceptible, but must be knowable. Anything that is knowable must be provable, hence accessible to all. As pointed out by Hegel, although in a different context, anything that is not knowable does not exist. Therefore, we have every reason to conclude that there is a knowable world, i.e. the

---

2. Often we get confused between the terms "empiricism" and "empirical." The former as a philosophical method is restricted to sense-experience alone, while the latter accommodates reason and experimentation along with observation. This is a popular method in science.

world in which we live. For a finite being it is this material world which is ultimately real. This is the point where the difference between physics and metaphysics disappears if we view it properly.

Elimination of Metaphysics

Owing their allegiance to the interpretation that metaphysics is a doctrine which deals with the entities that do not come under the purview of sensory experience, logical positivists want to eliminate metaphysics from the sphere of philosophy. But the consequences of the project, namely, the elimination of metaphysics proved too costly for logical positivists. It will be revealed in the course of its inquiry. However, the project undertaken by logical positivists is not all that new in the history of philosophy. As we have shown in the first chapter, Hume consigns all metaphysics to flames for it can contain nothing but "sophistry and illusion." Even Immanuel Kant (1724-1804), at least in one phase of his work *Critique of Pure Reason* attempts to show that "metaphysics" of a certain sort is impossible. According to Kant, the human understanding can grasp only what can be experienced. For Kant, the term "experience" includes both formal element (categories of understanding) and material element (the information supplied by the senses). But reason, holds Kant, strives to go beyond the confines of the understanding to conceive the supersensible for which we have no object in perception. To quote Kant's remarks in this context:

> Metaphysics is a completely isolated speculative science of reason, which soars far above the teachings of experience, and in which reason is indeed meant to be its own pupil.[3]

Thus Kant argues that we cannot have knowledge of the

3. Immanuel Kant, *Critique of Pure Reason*, tr. Norman Kemp Smith, (London, 1973), p. 21.

supersensible,[4] because our knowledge is confined to the world of phenomena only, whereas the neumenal entities transcend our sphere of knowledge. This is what Kant says about the impossibility of a certain sort of metaphysics. In the early nineteenth century Auguste Comte (1798-1857), a well-known French positivist, attempted to show that metaphysics is one of the stages of man's intellectual development. It is, according to Comte, a speculative doctrine concerning the "essences" and "causes" of phenomena. Comte claims to have rejected metaphysics as a stage on the way to positive knowledge and it (positivist stage) is the stage from where the world has outgrown. Comte envisages that positivist stage is the culmination of the evolution of human thought, which had passed from the "theological stage" to the "metaphysical stage" and then to the "positive stage." At the first stage, Comte assumes that reality is made dependent on divine beings; at the second, these religious ideas have been replaced by speculative thinking about natural phenomena, and at the third stage, the human mind recognises the impossibility of acquiring absolute knowledge and gives up the idea of investigating the origin and purpose of the universe. For Comte considers that the sole object of science is to discover natural laws or the constant relations existing between the facts and this can be done only by observation and experience. Knowledge thus acquired, claims Comte, is positive knowledge and only such knowledge can be successfully applied to various fields of human practice as is verified by positive sciences.[5] In this way,

4. Kant uses the word "supersensible" to denote "things-in-themselves." According to him, we cannot have universal and necessary or a priori knowledge of anything non-perceivable. Hence, we cannot have knowledge of metaphysics that transcends experience. The metaphysics of "things-in-themselves" include free will, immortality, and God. They exist only in a noumenal realm.

5. F. Mayer, *A History of Modern Philosophy* (New Delhi, 1976), pp. 404-8.

for Comte, metaphysics deals with the "essences and causes" of the universe. As a matter of fact, logical positivist conception of natural sciences is akin to that of Hume and Auguste Comte. Both Hume and Comte regard natural science as something that is concerned with ordering of sensory experiences which ultimately result in positive facts. It is these objects of sensations which have been differently designated by these philosophers. Hume's pure sensationalism and his rejection of metaphysics of transcendental kind have been adopted by logical positivists in a different style. Here, we shall confine ourselves to the doctrine of A.J. Ayer.

Ayer, in defence of logical positivist tenets, proclaims that the reason to oppose metaphysics is that metaphysicians always try to explain reality as a whole and attempt to describe super-sensible world in such a way as if it were given to sensory experience. In this sense, holds Ayer, metaphysics is not only speculative but also nonsensical. To quote Ayer's remarks on metaphysics:

> The positivist flavour of their thought comes out most strongly in their hostility to metaphysics. Metaphysics, which they construed as covering such allegedly philosophical enterprises as the attempt to describe Reality as a whole, or to find the purpose of Universe, or to reach beyond the everyday world to some supra-sensible spiritual order, was condemned by them not as being unduly speculative, or even as being false, but as being literally nonsensical.[6]

Being ardent followers of empiricist principles, logical positivists assert that it is impossible to go beyond sensory experiences. Apart from this, they consider nature or reality as an arbitrary collection of sense-experiences. This aspect will be given due consideration in Ayer's theory of perception.

---

6. A.J. Ayer, "The Vienna Circle", in his *The Revolution in Philosophy*, p. 74.

Sharing his hostility towards metaphysics with other logical positivists, Ayer questions the veracity of metaphysical statements. What are the premises from which the statements of metaphysics are deduced? What kind of reasoning does lead a metaphysician to arrive at such conclusions? Ayer remarks that there is no other way for a metaphysician except empirical verification to infer anything about the nature of the reality. But a metaphysician might say that "he was endowed with a faculty of intellectual intuition which enabled him to know facts that could not be known through sense-experience."[7] A metaphysician might think that it is a legitimate method to approach the reality of transcendental kind. Perhaps, Ayer feels that it is not an easy task to overthrow his claim that the transcendental nature of reality is derived from the premises supplied by intellectual intuition. The only alternative left for Ayer is to attack metaphysicians on logical grounds. This is where Ayer and other logical positivists claim to add logical rigour to the traditional empiricism of Hume. Ayer argues that:

> Our charge against the metaphysician is not that he attempts to employ the understanding in a field where it cannot profitably venture, but that he produces sentences which fail to conform to the conditions under which alone a sentence can be literally significant.[8]

Thus Ayer provides a linguistic turn to the problems related to metaphysics. Even in this case Ayer's interests do not appear to be safe because a metaphysician might claim that the statements of metaphysics conform to the conditions stipulated by him. So it is not a happy hunting ground for an avowed empiricist like Ayer to venture into the field of metaphysics. In spite of all these impediments, Ayer puts forward a criterion which would enable him to distinguish meaningful statements

7. A.J. Ayer, *Language, Truth and Logic*, p. 46.

8. Ibid., p. 47.

(propositions) from the meaningless assertions of metaphysics. In an attempt to justify his claim, Ayer introduces the "principles of verification" as a criterion of meaning.

The Wedge between Analytic and Synthetic

In order to provide a detailed account of verification principle, that is supposed to furnish a criterion through which meaningful statements[9] are separated from meaningless assertions, there is every need to know the history of the classification of propositions into two important types, namely, the propositions of exact sciences like mathematics and logic and the propositions of natural sciences. We have already discussed in our first chapter that Hume made a valiant attempt to get rid of transcendental metaphysics with his supposed fork between relations of ideas and matters of fact. Hume proposes that any reasoning, whatsoever it may be, should either terminate in sensory experience or could be defined in terms of ideas of reason. If any reasoning does not abide by this condition, says Hume, it is considered metaphysical. All metaphysical statements, according to Hume, exhibit only "sophistry and illusion." If we substitute the word "meaninglessness" for the phrase "sophistry and illusion," we shall have the logical positivist doctrine. We shall show that logical positivists converted the epistemological doctrine of Hume into a semantic one.

---

9. Ayer distinguishes "statements" from "propositions." In the introduction of his book *Language, Truth and Logic,* he writes that what is expressed by an "indicative sentence" is called a statement. In other words, a statement is regarded as what is expressed by a sentence irrespective of its meaningfulness. In this sense all "metaphysical" utterances come under the category of statements. The phrase "indicative" is used by Ayer to refer to a particular aspect. For instance, the sentence "God is omnipresent" is indicating a particular quality of God. Whereas a proposition is that which expresses a meaningful statement.

Like Hume, Ayer too classified important propositions into analytic and synthetic. The former class (relations of ideas) comprises the "analytic" propositions of logic and mathematics, which are a priori (independent of sensory experience), and analytic (tautologies) in their nature; the latter class (matters of fact) comprises empirical propositions of everyday science and are a posteriori (derived from sense-experience). The propositions of logic and mathematics are tautologies because:

> . . . they are independent of experience in the sense that they do not owe their validity to empirical verification. We may come to discover them through an inductive process; but once we have apprehended them we see that they are necessarily true, that they hold good for every conceivable instance.[10]

According to the above statement of Ayer, the statements of logic and mathematics are derived through inductive method. In fact, this is the position of J.S. Mill. It is a well-known fact that any proposition derived through induction cannot be necessary and certain. Maybe Ayer used it by mistake. Otherwise what follows from the above quotation of Ayer is that the propositions of logic and mathematics are purely verbal conventions and their truths are discovered by a priori reasoning alone. There is also another possibility that Ayer uses the term "inductive" in the sense that in the inductive reasoning we proceed from particulars to generalisations. For instance, the proposition 2+3 = 5 is a particular instance from which we can generalise that in all the instances of the similar kind 2+3 = 5. These truths cannot be refuted by sense-experience. However, it is a contradiction from the standpoint of logic to say that induction involves a priorism. The synthetic propositions of natural science, on the other hand, are not universal and necessary since any future sense-experience can

---

10. A.J. Ayer, *Language, Truth and Logic*, p. 100.

confute a well established truth of an empirical generalisation. To this effect they are highly probable.

Even Kant made a sharp distinction between "analytic" and "synthetic" judgements. For he considers that this distinction is necessary because genuine knowledge always appears in the form of synthetic judgements[11] a priori in which something is affirmed or denied. However, every judgement does not fulfil this criterion. In an analytic judgement the predicate merely expresses what is already "contained" in the subject. For example, "Body is an extended thing" is an analytic judgement as the quality of "extension" is inseparable from the body. It is imperative that to be a body it has to have extension. Similarly, the example "A triangle contains three interior angles" expresses that the notion of "three angles" is implied in the concept of a triangle. On the contrary, a synthetic judgement is a judgement, holds Kant, in which the predicate adds something new to the subject. For example, "All bodies have specific gravity" expresses a unique quality of objects which is not inherent in the bodies.[12] This is to say that a body does not cease to be a body in the absence of specific gravity. This is purely an extraneous factor imposed on bodies because of earth's gravitational pull. Bodies tend to have levitation once they go beyond the limits of gravitational pull of the earth. However, Kant maintains that synthetic judgements cannot be regarded as informers of genuine knowledge unless they are organised by the categories of understanding (formal element or concepts)

---

11. Kant's use of the term "Judgement" has a special meaning. Prima facie, a judgement appears to be a proposition but it is not. A proposition may be a true assertion of a fact. Unlike a proposition, a judgement involves reasoning based on experience. Therefore in Kantian philosophy a judgement is not identical with a proposition. In other words, a judgement is the mediate knowledge of an object in question.

12. Immanuel Kant, *Critique of Pure Reason*, pp. 48-51.

and forms of intuition (space and time). Mind, maintains Kant, possesses a priori forms of understanding which organise the manifold of data furnished by sensory experience. Thus he emphasises, "Concepts without percepts are empty, percepts without concepts are blind."[13] Accordingly, thoughts without the admixture of sensory data, and sensory experience without a priori forms of understanding do not contain knowledge at all. Knowledge, for Kant, consists in "synthetic judgements a priori." Unlike Hume, Kant treats the judgements of mathematics as *synthetic* a priori. For instance, the proposition 7+5 = 12 is not only synthetic but also a priori. It is synthetic, according to Kant, because the predicate 12 is not in 7 or 5 but the combination of both with the symbol + (plus) gives something new. They are a priori because 7+5 is "necessarily" followed by 12. It is important to note here that Kant's use of the term a priori is not identical or synonymous to analytic. A priori is the mark of necessity in Kant's scheme philosophy.

Trying to vindicate how his (Ayer's) approach differs from that of Kant with regard to analytic/synthetic distinction, Ayer maintains that Kant's account of the cleavage between analytic and synthetic propositions is not clear because Kant could not give one straightforward criterion for this separation. Ayer says that Kant employs a psychological criterion for holding that the propositions of mathematics are both synthetic and a priori, while his ground for holding that the proposition "All bodies are extended" rests upon the principle of non-contradiction alone. In this way, Kant, argues Ayer, uses psychological criterion in the case of synthetic propositions and logical criterion in the case of analytic propositions.[14] Ayer argues that the above-said criterion of Kant allows certain propositions to trade between analytic and synthetic. For

---

13. Immanuel Kant, op. cit., p. 93.

14. A.J. Ayer, *Language, Truth and Logic*, p. 104.

instance, a proposition which is synthetic according to psychological criterion may very well be analytic according to logical criterion. Nevertheless, Ayer recognises the epistemological importance of Kant's cleavage between analytic and synthetic judgements.

Kant's approach towards the classification of judgements into analytic and synthetic appears more rational than psychological in the sense that he is very scrupulous in identifying the propositions of mathematics with other propositions of natural science; for example, the proposition "7+5 = 12" is not only necessary, but also informative. The various permutations and combinations of the mathematical symbols result in different value structures of the mathematical propositions. One does not know whether these value structures are inherent in their respective combinations in question, unless one knows the schemes, methods and techniques involved in mathematical sciences. In this sense, perhaps, what Kant says is not only rational but can also be acceptable without much ado. Above all, the propositions of mathematics like propositions of natural sciences involve experience. Here it is important to note that the term "experience" should not be taken in its parochial sense, namely, sense-experience.

In support of Hume and in contrast to Kant, Ayer puts forward the view that "a proposition is analytic when its validity depends solely on the definitions of the symbols it contains, and synthetic when its validity is determined by the facts of experience."[15] To this extent Ayer is in agreement with Hume and Kant. The validity of any analytic proposition is solely dependent on its definitions. Hence, they are verbal. But, the validity of a synthetic statement is dependent on the sensory experience. Ayer disagrees with Kant with regard to the status of the statements of mathematics and logic. Unlike

15. A.J. Ayer, *Language, Truth and Logic*, p. 105.

Kant and like Hume, Ayer maintains that all the statements of mathematics and logic are analytic since they are verbal conventions. Their values are not variable. Thus all meaningful statements for Ayer exhaust in between these two categories. The very reason to demarcate, as it is held by Ayer, analytical propositions from synthetic ones is to isolate metaphysical assertions from meaningful ones.

The Principle of Verification

Once the demarcation between analytic and synthetic propositions is complete, logical positivists more or less took it for granted that their important task of getting rid of metaphysical statements as meaningless is successful. But it is so unfortunate that they could not realise the sharp razor consequences that were in offing which led to water down version of the principle of verification. Moritz Schlick defines verification as: "The meaning of a statement is the method of its verification."[16] What Schlick means by this definition is that the meaning of a statement in question can be established if one knows under what conditions a statement is empirically verifiable. Ayer redefines verification principle in the following manner:

> The principle of verification is supposed to furnish a criterion by which it can be determined whether or not a sentence is literally meaningful. A simple way to formulate it would be to say that a sentence had literal meaning if and only if the proposition it expressed was either analytic or empirically verifiable.[17]

Thus it is the method through which "meaningful" statements are separated from "meaningless" assertions. The biconditional

16. Moritz Schlick, "Positivism and Realism", in A.J. Ayer (ed.), *Logical Positivism.*
17. A.J. Ayer, *Language, Truth and Logic*, p. 7

nature of this method is that it would ascribe "literal" meaning only to those statements which are either truisms (self-evident truths) or empirically verifiable. Proceeding further Ayer states: "We say that a sentence is factually significant to any given person, if and only if he knows how to verify the proposition which it purports to express — that is, if he knows what observations would lead him, under certain conditions, to accept the proposition as being true, or reject it as being false."[18]

In the first instance it can be seen as an attempt to eliminate metaphysical statements as nonsensical. It can be deduced from the above quotation of Ayer that the statement expressed by any sentence is held to be meaningful in so far as one knows how to verify it with his sense-experience. The statements which could not meet this standard are regarded as meaningless and consequently metaphysical. But a special exception has been made in favour of analytic statements of mathematics and logic. The so-called Ockham's razor of logical positivists (principle of verification) is not applicable to analytic statements since they are self-evidently true.

Ayer tries to distinguish his use of the word "meaning" from other uses. The word "meaning," says Ayer, has different meanings in philosophy. In some cases a statement is said to be meaningful even if it does not fulfil the requirements of verification principle. Ayer maintains, however, there is one proper use of the word "meaning" in which it would not be correct to say that a statement is meaningful unless it satisfies the verification theory. Precisely this is the reason, claims Ayer, why he uses the expression "literal meaning" to distinguish it from other uses.[19] According to Ayer, "literal meaning" is derived from "factual meaning." A statement is factually meaningful if it is empirically verifiable. Consequently, a statement is literally meaningful if it is factually meaningful.

18. A.J. Ayer, *Language, Truth and Logic*, p. 48.

19. Ibid., p. 20.

For example, the statement "Arsenic is a poisonous substance" has factual meaning since it is empirically verifiable. Here, Ayer's use of the expression "factual meaning" is identical with truth. In other words, if a statement is true, then it has literal meaning. Thus truth is identified with meaning. It is the process of verification that provides condition for truth.

Ayer makes a sharp distinction between the "strong" and the "weak" sense of the term "verifiability." The reason is that if the principle of verification is applied in its original form it would turn not only the statements of metaphysics as nonsensical, but it would also render (1) universal generalisations, (2) statements about the past, and (3) statements of natural science equally nonsensical, since none of the above-said statements is ever conclusively verifiable. In order to overcome this difficulty Ayer introduced this classification. According to Ayer:

> A proposition is said to be verifiable, in the strong sense of the term, if, and only if, its truth could be conclusively established in experience. But it is verifiable, in the weak sense, if it is possible for experience to render it probable.[20]

Even in its amended form it appears that the term "strong sense" refers to conclusive verifiability. In that case to what end does this classification serve the purpose? The only alternative left for us is to employ verification principle in its mitigated form (weak sense). Trying to clarify the exact nature of conclusive verifiability in its amended form of the principle, Ayer claims that the term "conclusive" is used in a different sense. Ayer feels that there are certain empirical propositions that can be verified conclusively in the sense that they are directly given in sense-experience. Anything that is given in one's own sense-experience is conclusively verified.[21] For

---

20. A.J. Ayer, *Language, Truth and Logic*, p. 50.

21. Ibid., p. 14.

example, the statement "There is X in the next room" could be verified conclusively in the Ayer's sense of the term "conclusive verifiability." If anybody wants to confirm whether it is true (meaningful) or not, he can verify the statement. This results in conclusive verification since a person trusts his own sensory experience. However, this will not solve the problem of universal generalisations. In fact, Schlick demanded for conclusive verifiability. If a proposition is not conclusively verifiable, argues Schlick, then it is not a proposition at all. In that case all generalisations of law become nonsensical, since they could neither be verified nor be confuted conclusively. With this the very purpose of verification principle is defeated. As Schlick points out we will have, then, nonsensical statements of metaphysics and important nonsensical statements of natural sciences.[22]

According to the "weak sense" of the term, a proposition is literally meaningful if there are some observations that would be relevant to its truth or falsity. This criterion, feels Ayer, would allow significance to the general propositions as it is clear that we can at least find evidence for or against them. In fact, Ayer identifies the "strong sense" of the term verification with "verification in practice" and "weak sense" of the term verification with "verification in principle." Much to Ayer's discomfort, the weak sense of the term "verification" allows every proposition to be meaningful irrespective of its status. Let us try the following criterion of Ayer whether it would satisfy the conditions of the verification principle.

> I propose to say that a statement is indirectly verifiable if it satisfies the following conditions; first, in conjunction with certain other premises — it entails one or more directly verifiable statements which are not deducible from these other

---

22. J.K. Weinberg, *An Examination of Logical Positivism* (London, 1936), p. 146.

> premises alone; and secondly that these other premises do not include any statement that is not either analytic, or directly verifiable or capable of being independently established as indirectly verifiable.[23]

The above quotation of Ayer painstakingly explains the nature of "weak sense" of the term "verifiability." This criterion meets with unfortunate consequences that it allows not only the statements of natural science as meaningful but also the statements of metaphysics. Let us take Ayer's own example to explain the weakness of this criterion. The statement (S) "The absolute is lazy" is the statement to be verified. The statement (O) "This is white" is an observation statement. "O" does not follow from either of the premises. It follows from the conjunction of "S" and if "S" then "O." Thus the statements "The absolute is lazy" and "If the absolute is lazy then this is white" jointly entail the statement "This is white." In this way any piece of nonsense can be rendered meaningful with this criterion. In fact, Alonzo Church pointed out this weakness with his ingenious technique. Church exposes the weakness of the principle in the following way.

Let "S" represent a nonsensical statement like "The nothing itself nothings." Then take any three logically independent observational statements O_1, O_2 and O_3.

O_1 represents "This is white"

O_2 represents "This is very strong"

O_3 represents "This is round"

The compound statement "C" of these three observational statements can be written in the following way:

Either (not — O_1 and O_2) or (O_3 and not — S)

This compound statement "C," according to Church, is certainly

23. A.J. Ayer, *Language, Truth and Logic*, p. 17.

verifiable because "C" taken together with O_1 entails O_3. But "C" taken together with "S" entails O_2. Therefore, according to Ayer's criterion, "S" must be verifiable, unless "S" entails O_2 on its own. But this cannot be the case since O_3 and not-S jointly entail O_2. Since O_3 and O_2 are logically independent, it follows that not-S is directly verifiable.[24] Although this is a complicated formula, it completely exposes the inherent contradictions that are involved in Ayer's criterion. Ayer concedes this in his later work *The Central Questions of Philosophy*.

There are several other interpretations of the principle of verification; since our main study is confined to the doctrine of A.J. Ayer we do not want to pay much heed to them. By and large, all the interpretations lead to the same negative conclusions. We must now, therefore, critically examine Ayer's principle of verification from different standpoints. The principle of verification is inseparably linked with the distinction between analytic and synthetic. If we can show this distinction as invalid then the verification principle would no longer be valid.

Critical Reflections

The most common and notable objection about the cleavage between analytic and synthetic comes from W.V. Quine. For he considers that the empiricism of logical positivists is largely conditioned by two important dogmas, namely, the belief in the supposed boundary between analytic and synthetic knowledge and reductionism. These two dogmas, according to Quine, are constructed on the vague structures of physical object language. He argues that the basic concept of logical positivism which regarded language to be the starting point of analysis is ill founded, since the so-called physical object language proposed by logical positivists is itself at variance with its own

24. Alonzo Church, "Review of the second edn. of *Language, Truth and Logic*", *Journal of Symbolic Logic* (London, 1949), XIV, pp. 52-53.

demand. In order to expose the pitfalls in their (logical positivists') approach, Quine adopts the following analysis.

First of all, there cannot be any precise definition of "analyticity" without presupposing the notion of analytic. What then is the notion of analytic? In search of a clear definition of analytic, Quine tries to identify analytic with "synonymity," "meaning," "definition," "interchangeability *salva veritate*" and "formation and transformation of linguistic rules." What Quine argues is that the term "analytic" can be interpreted in all these ways, but he comes to the conclusion that in all these cases it is necessary to appeal to an a priori use of "analyticity." To start with the Frege's notion that meaning cannot be identified with naming, for example, "evening star and morning star," since these two terms may mean the same object, i.e. the planet Venus, but their meaning is treated as distinct. If both these terms, holds Quine, were alike in the meaning, then the identity "Evening star = Morning Star" would be analytic.[25]

Quine classifies analytic statements into two categories. The first class is called logically true propositions. For example, "No unmarried man is married." The important feature of this example, says Quine, is that it remains true under any reinterpretation of the terms "man" and "married." The other class of analytic statements like, "No bachelor is married" can be converted into logically true statements by providing synonyms for synonyms. In this way, the statement "No bachelor is married" can be translated into "No unmarried man is married" by providing "unmarried man" for its synonym "bachelor." Nevertheless, maintains Quine, we are lacking proper criterion to characterise the second class of analytic statements, i.e. analyticity as such because we tend to say that a statement is analytic, if the relevant terms are synonymous.

25. W.V. Quine, "Two Dogmas of Empiricism", in *Problems in the Philosophy of Language*, ed. Thomas M. Olschewsky (London, 1969), p. 399.

But what is synonymy? This question, says Quine, leads us to the definition of logical truths. Quine asks the question how does one know that "bachelor" is defined as "unmarried man?" He supposes that it is a common practice to refer to the nearest dictionary. Quine says that he does not accept lexicographer's formulation as a law because lexicographer is an empirical scientist who records antecedent facts. Suppose, he glosses the term "bachelor" as "unmarried man" because it is lexicographer's belief that there is a relation of synonymy between these two forms. Even in this case, according to Quine:

> The notion of synonymy presupposed here has still to be clarified, presumably in terms relating to linguistic behaviour. Certainly the "definition" which is the lexicographer's report of an observed synonymy cannot be taken as the ground for synonymy.[26]

What follows from this statement of Quine is that to determine synonymity one has to depend upon empirical facts. In this way Quine tries to prove that the intentional circle is vacuous. If the words can only be defined in terms of each other, then they depend upon synthetic knowledge. It is true, admits Quine, that some terms can be defined in terms of others, in which case these latter terms are basic terms. Here it is important to notice that these terms cannot be explained or defined in the same way as the less basic terms, since they have a different logical status. It logically follows, thus, that no sentence has significance unless this significance is explained by references to others and ultimately on linguistic behaviour. Quine believes that it is enough to show that the supposed boundary between analytic and synthetic is an invalid one.

Quine is an empiricist in his own right. He believes that all the knowledge concerning natural, physical and mathematical sciences is "a man-made fabric." All knowledge, in one way or

26. W.V. Quine, op. cit., p. 402.

the other, is dependent on experience. He conceives that there are no propositions in science that are immune to revision. According to Quine, revision and redistribution of certain truth values affect the entire structure of the science as it (scientific knowledge) is an interconnected network.[27]

As pointed out by Quine, the distinction between analytic and synthetic is very superficial in scientific knowledge since knowledge is a synthesis of linguistic conceptual apparatus and experience. Experience in turn represents both theoretical and practical aspects of knowledge. Language and logic are inseparable from reality. The conventional truths of mathematical sciences are in one way the products of experience. They have their origin in reality. The universal nature of mathematical sciences is designed by men to know the quantitative structures of reality. Although they are the matters of convention, the validity and utility of mathematics lies in its application to empirical reality. Otherwise mathematics would become part of metaphysics if it is regarded as an abstract science that deals with the numbers and axioms. For instance, it is now very difficult to find a field of knowledge where mathematical methods and research approaches are not used. Mathematics is now becoming one of the powerful instruments in ascertaining the knowledge of reality. In appreciation of mathematical knowledge, Peter Caws writes in the following manner:

> Mathematics, which among the other things, is the study of numbers and their properties, has therefore exerted a great influence on the development of philosophy, and its already strong position among intellectual activities was enormously strengthened when it proved to be one of the most important factors in the development of science also. Only when Galileo turned his attention to accurate quantitative determinations did the laws of mechanics begin to be apparent, and he was

27. W.V. Quine, op. cit., p. 414.

> so impressed by this fact that he said that the "book of nature" was written in the language of mathematics.[28]

The relationship between mathematics and natural sciences is a well established one. Why then mathematics is relevant to philosophy? Yes, it is. Mathematical logic is one of the branches of philosophy. It is very important because mathematical logic being logic in subject matter and mathematics in method exerts a stupendous influence on generalising the ideas, concepts, and the language of mathematics itself. The successful development of mathematical logic and its impact on other sciences has brought about a revolution in the field of modern science in the form of artificial intelligence (computer technology). It is obvious from the above account of mathematical knowledge that the supposed distinction between analytic and synthetic does not have any firm ground to support itself.

Apart from the above criticism, the principle of verification has a number of curious and interesting features which can be criticised from various directions. The most curious among these is the question: Is verification principle an empirical proposition or a tautology? If it is neither, what, then, is its status? This is an interesting question that comes from John Wisdom. He comments:

> Well, shall we accept the verification principle? What is it to accept it? When people bring out with a dashing air of the words "The meaning of a statement is really simply the method of its verification, like one who says The value of a thing is really simply its power of exchange," in what sort of way are they using words? What is the general nature of their theory? The answer is: it is a metaphysical theory.[29]

---

28. Peter Caws, *The Philosophy of Science* (New York, 1965), p. 143.
29. John Wisdom, "Metaphysics and Verification", *Mind*, N.S., vol. XLVII, no. 47, 1936, p. 454.

This follows, according to Wisdom, that the principle of verification has been formulated in such a way that its purpose and nature is not clear. On the face of it, the principle by itself is neither empirically verifiable nor a tautology. Then it is one of those utterances of metaphysics.

Almost a similar kind of attack comes from Urmson.[30] He argues that the question regarding the status of the principle of verification has two possible answers from the standpoint of a positivist, namely, it is empirical, and it is a tautology (a rule of language). But, contests Urmson, it is not possible to show that the principle of verification belongs to either of the above-said categories on the following grounds. For logical positivists the statements of philosophy are not empirical, but only tautological clarifications of language. Apart from that, logical positivists did not go for an exhaustive study of all the metaphysical statements to show that they are meaningless independent of the principle of verification. Are they then prepared to examine all the statements of metaphysics to show that at least one metaphysical statement is an exception and is meaningful? They have relied on a few instances and concluded that all the statements of metaphysics are meaningless. Urmson's arguments are very logical. It is completely ruled out that the principle of verification is an empirical formulation. If it were to be considered as a rule of language of a conventional character (a priori), the critics of the principle might say that the word "meaningful" would be used in a sense that it brings entire metaphysics under the fold of meaningfulness.

G.J. Warnock, on the other hand, illustrates that we ordinarily inquire into semantics of words or sentences. According to logicians, a proposition is articulated in the sense

30. J.O. Urmson, *Philosophical Analysis between Two World Wars* (London, 1971), pp. 168-69.

that it expresses what a sentence means. In this sense a proposition is not something which has meaning. Warnock argues that according to the principle of verification, it is propositions which we verify and describe whether they are true or false. Then we cannot, says Warnock, speak of meaning of a sentence, or of the meaning of what a sentence stands for. To avoid this confusion, Warnock suggests the epigram should be modified as "The meaning of a sentence is the method of its verification."[31]

Proceeding further, Warnock holds that whenever we talk about verification of a statement, it is somehow connected with truth or falsity. For example, to verify "P" is to find out whether "P" is true or not. But there are, argues Warnock, certain meaningful sentences which do not have any concern with truth or falsity. With a view to explaining the nature of such meaningful sentences that are not in need of verification, Warnock says:

> They are imperative sentences, used (mainly) to give orders; and interrogative sentences, used (mainly) to ask questions. There are sentences used as prayers; to make promises; to give verdicts; to express decisions; to pass moral judgements; or to make proposals. It is nonsensical to ask of a question, an order, a prayer, or a proposal, whether it is true or false. . . .[32]

The questions posed by Warnock further kills the spirit of verification principle, if at all there is any, of logical positivists. It does not make sense to speak of verification of commands, prayers, promises, expressions of wishes, etc. Even if one wishes to say that they are meaningless, according to the principle of verification, it is only a trivial remark which does not harm their linguistic respectability. Thus Warnock concludes that

31. G.J. Warnock, "Verification and Use of Language", in *Problems in the Philosophy of Language*, ed. Thomas M. Olshewsky, p. 184.

32. Ibid., pp. 184-85.

non-satisfaction of the principle of verification does not necessarily result in "meaninglessness."

The other important issue, for Warnock, is the notion of "verifiability" itself. Warnock believes that the phrase "method of verification" is somewhat misleading. What does it mean when we speak of methods of verification? Trying to show the vagueness of the term "method of verification" of logical positivists, Warnock argues that the methods adopted by statisticians, chemists and painters differ in their approaches in accordance with their subject matter. There is not even single method, argues Warnock, which would satisfy all of them.[33] According to Warnock, there is no fixed method of verification. The method of verification is proper within the purview of specialists, scientists, statisticians, doctors, even detectives, etc. but not in our daily conversation. In the similar fashion a metaphysician could also claim that he applies his own method of verification to establish that the statements of metaphysics are true or false (meaningful).

Karl Popper, a well-known philosopher of science who is often mistaken as a follower of logical positivism, introduces the method of falsification in place of logical positivists' verification principle. However, Popper's intentions are something different from those of logical positivists'. Unlike logical positivists, Popper is interested in demarcating science from pseudo-science. Though some say that Popper's programme is similar to that of logical positivists', it is obvious that Popper is more interested in epistemological considerations rather than in semantic ones. Popper conceives that the business of philosophy of science is to inquire into the nature of the method which a scientist employs, as well as its rationality. In order to show this, Popper raises the question: What is a scientific theory? His answer is that a theory is scientific only

33. G.J. Warnock, op. cit., p. 188.

in so far as it is falsifiable or refutable.[34] His criterion is not to be misunderstood. Prima facie it appears that Popper's theory is paradoxical. Popper does not mean to say that a scientific theory is one which gets refuted or falsified. He only means to say that a scientific theory forbids certain states of affair. For example, the statement "Arsenic is a poisonous substance" is a scientific theory in the sense that it forbids the quality of non-poisonous character of arsenic. Thus it gives chance for falsifiability or refutability. On the other hand, statements of pseudo-science (metaphysics) do not forbid any states of affair. Hence, they are not falsifiable. Popper's main intention in introducing falsifiability, as a criterion is not only to demarcate science from pseudo-science, but also to reduce the number of contending hypotheses for explaining a class of phenomena.

In retaliation to Popper's theory of falsifiability, Ayer claims that conclusive falsifiability is as good as conclusive verifiability. Ayer believes that since all the statements of science are not directly observable, some provision must be made for indirect falsification. Then it is in no way better than indirect verification because it cannot escape from Church's formula.[35]

Gilbert Ryle writes that in the epigram "the meaning of a proposition is the method of its verification," the word "proposition" was made to cover not just statements of natural law (scientific statements) but statements of all kinds. He tries to differentiate statements of law from conjectural statements. The word "hypothesis," he supposes, is used ambiguously in many cases. Ryle contends that the term "hypothesis" has two different uses. It is used to denote any true or false statement of law, i.e. any variable hypothetical statement of the kind "whenever . . ., then," and also to refer to any conjectural

34. Karl Popper, *The Logic of Scientific Discovery* (London, 1980), pp. 40-42.

35. A.J. Ayer, The *Central Questions of Philosophy*, pp. 27-28.

statement whatever it may be. For example, the statement "My neighbour is in pain" is not a statement of law, since the statements of law cannot be proved true or false. It is only a conjectural statement. In that case, argues Ryle, the principle of verification should be applied to conjectural statements but not to the statements of law. Ryle feels that the statements of science are not to be put for the test of verification or falsification since they are well-established truths. The generalised version of the principle is too narrow that it tries to impose the test of validity not only on the non-scientific statements but also on the valid scientific laws. Thus Ryle attacks both verification and falsification.[36]

It is so unfortunate that the principle of verification, which was introduced by logical positivists with a good intention of purifying philosophy could not withstand grave objections. Another weakness of the principle of verification is that it dismisses all the statements of social activity as meaningless. Verification in the first place is not mere sensory experience but a practical activity that involves some interaction between a person and his surroundings. The person who is verifying a proposition in question performs an action or series of actions. For example, scientists verify the properties of various substances. It is not necessary that all the properties are sense-given. There are many properties inherent in the substances that are to be known experimentally. Experimentation invariably involves reasoning, observation, practical activity and hypothesis formation. A scientist does not solely depend on sensory experience (observation) to inquire into the processes of reality. But, for Ayer and other logical positivists verification means to have certain sort of sensations. These sensations cannot go beyond the appearances. The inner

36. G. Ryle, "The Verification Principle", in his *Collected Papers* (London, 1971), p. 290.

structures of phenomena (essences) are not given in sensory experience but known through experimentation. In fact, the principle of verification of Ayer misinterprets the concepts such as "knowledge" and "experience." According to Ayer, "knowledge" is acquired through sensing one's own sensations. This position of Ayer boils down to solipsism. The verification principle of Ayer, in the ultimate analysis, rests on the processes to which all sense-given objects are related.

II

Although the principle of verification is shown to be inconsistent with its own formulations, its impact on value statements is something unpalatable. The question arises: If according to the principle of verification only empirical and analytical statements are meaningful, what then would be the fate of value statements? Since the value statements are not verifiable, it logically follows that they are meaningless. In order to escape from this drastic conclusion, Ayer holds that value statements are not meaningless but emotive in their nature. Before going to discuss the semantic status of value statements, first we will discuss what values are. Primarily, the statements of ethics, religion and aesthetics are brought under this category. In an attempt to prove that the statements of religion and aesthetics are pseudo-statements, logical positivists introduced the principle of verification. But, the natural consequence of such an exercise is that even the statements of ethics are also treated on a par with the statements of religion and aesthetics.

What are Values?

Values are properties of objects and social phenomena that determine their importance to society or to a class of individuals. The theory of values is concerned with what things or social phenomena are good, desirable and important to human individuals. Things or objects represent the various and different types of value since they are the objects of different human interests. Broadly speaking, values can be classified into material and non-material ones. For instance, a pot being a vessel possesses material value, i.e. a use value. As a product of human design the pot has aesthetic as well as economic value too. But in all these relationships a pot appears not merely as a material object but an artefact of humankind as well. The most important of non-material values are moral values. Actions of people in certain social set-up represent moral, good or evil. Thus, values are objects of approval or condemnation. To direct and regulate the conduct of people, society erects a system of ethical concepts, ideals, principles and assessment. These moral values constitute the very essence of a "just society." This does not mean that value system in a society is a static phenomenon. The vicissitudes of time bring about drastic changes in the value system of a given society. Otherwise an immutable value system in the society is the sign of decadence in value system. Ethical values are the sum total of standards or rules of conduct reflecting peoples' ideas of justice and injustice, good and evil. The ethical standards are maintained by the approbation of public opinion, customs, habits and education but not by mere force of individual's convictions. Let us now confine ourselves to the moral values as expounded by Ayer in his "emotive theory of ethics."

Types of Ethical Theory

Ayer points out that ordinary system of ethics, as discussed in the doctrines of moralists, is an amalgam of utterances of metaphysics, and unfruitful analyses of non-ethical concepts. He intends to classify them into four important categories. The first class, says Ayer, consists of propositions that express definitions of ethical terms or judgements and about the legitimacy or possibility of certain definitions. Secondly, there are propositions that describe the phenomena of moral experience, and their causes. Thirdly, there are exhortations to moral virtue. Finally, there are actual ethical judgements.

Of all these four classes of propositions, claims Ayer, the first category of propositions, in which an ethical term is used in a purely normative way, is said to constitute ethical philosophy. Only such propositions constitute the genuine ethical philosophy. Ayer develops his "emotive theory of values" from those propositions alone. The other three classes of propositions are not to be considered as parts of ethical philosophy on the grounds that the second class of propositions (the propositions which describe the nature of moral experience) belongs to the science of psychology or sociology. The third class of propositions (the exhortations to moral virtue) does not belong to any science. The actual ethical judgements that belong to fourth class are not definitions or comments upon definitions or quotations. In the strict sense moral philosophy does not contain declarations or announcements.[37]

Emotive Theory

Since moral statements cannot be directly verified by appeal to sense-experience, Ayer considers the possibility whether moral statements can be translated into statements that can be so verified without any loss in their meaning. If this possibility is within the reach, says Ayer, then the moral statements are fit to be qualified, though not immediately, as meaningful. Consequently, they belong to empirical statements. With a view to confirming the possibility of this claim, Ayer attempts to analyse two versions of this view, namely, subjectivism and utilitarianism.

Subjectivists, argues Ayer, hold that an action is true or right because it is generally approved of, or alternatively that it is approved by the speaker. Ayer rejects this view on the ground that it cannot mean the same to say the one as to say the other, since it can be accepted without contradiction to say of something that is both generally approved of and wrong.

37. A.J. Ayer, *Language, Truth and Logic*, p. 137.

For example, the assertion "Bonded labour is a crime" is right because it received approbation from the public, but the same assertion can be wrong even if it received public approbation. Ayer, therefore, rejects the possibility that ethical predicates such as "good," "right" or "virtue" can ever be translated into empirical predicates "approved by all" or "approved by me." On exactly the same grounds he rejects utilitarianism. According to this theory, moral virtue lies in "the greatest happiness to the greatest number." In this case, an action is regarded right since it is accepted by the majority. Ayer believes that it is not a contradiction to say that an action is sometimes wrong to perform which would cause the greatest happiness. What Ayer tries to clarify is "right action" and "action causing the greatest happiness" cannot mean the same thing. It amounts to saying that "it is sometimes wrong to perform the right action."[38] Then there is no possibility of translating ethical terms into empirical ones.

Absolutists, on the other hand, argue that their ethical considerations are based on "the view that statements of value are not controlled by observation, as ordinary empirical propositions are, but only by mysterious "intellectual intuition."[39] This claim is akin to that of metaphysicians. If the statements of ethics, as claimed by absolutists, are non-empirical then they are either analytic or nonsensical. Ayer opines that they cannot be analytical since they are the products of "intellectual intuition." On this ground Ayer rejects absolutism too and adopts a third theory which he calls "emotive theory." According to this theory, ethical concepts are unanalysable since they are pseudo-concepts. They are, in the view of Ayer, statements of a different kind. Ayer envisages that the predicates used in value statements are not proper since they

38. A.J. Ayer, *Language, Truth and Logic*, pp. 138-39.

39. Ibid., p. 140.

do not stand for any qualities that can be given in sense-experience.[40] Proceeding further, Ayer holds:

> The presence of an ethical symbol on a proposition adds nothing to its factual content. Thus if I say to some one, "you acted wrongly in stealing that money," I am not stating anything more than if I had simply said: "you stole that money." In adding that this action is wrong I am not making any further statement about it. I am simply evincing my moral disapproval of it. It is as if I had said, "you stole that money," in a peculiar tone of horror, or written it with the addition of some special exclamation marks. The tone, or the exclamation marks, add nothing to the literal meaning of the sentence. It merely serves to show that the expression of it is attended by certain feelings in the speaker.[41]

What follows from this theory is that statements of value do not qualify as meaningful as they are mere expressions of sentiments or emotions of the speaker in question. They appear to be the expressions of a fact, but in real sense they are not. In this way, they are in no way different from metaphysical assertions. But, Ayer does not want to dismiss them (statements of ethics) as meaningless. He assigns a different function to value statements. He argues:

> . . . it is advisable to put them into a separate category altogether; either to say that they are not to be counted as statements at all, if this proves inconvenient, at least to say that they do not express propositions, and consequently there are no ethical facts.[42]

It amounts to saying that the statements of ethics do not have any objective significance. In fact, Ayer's doctrine of morality

---

40. A.J. Ayer, *Language, Truth and Logic*, p. 141.

41. Ibid., p. 142.

42. A.J. Ayer, "On the Analysis of Moral Judgements", in his *Philosophical Essays*, pp. 232-33.

is an extreme form of subjectivism. It is ridiculous to say that we do not assert any statements about morals. Then, what would be the fate of a society? It would become another non-entity since statements about social relationships are pseudo-statements. Ayer concludes that moral judgements are emotive rather than descriptive. They are only expressions of attitudes of individuals. Since they are not the statements of facts, truth or falsity cannot be ascribed to them.[43] Ayer reasserts his position when he says that one may feel strong moral indignation but moral principles "are autonomous. You cannot in the last resort justify your moral standpoint in terms of anything else."[44] Accordingly, the above statements of Ayer are merely his own emotions. Actually they do not correspond to anything in reality.

It is unbecoming of a philosopher like Ayer to shun all the aspects related to social reality as they do not comply with the principle of verification. In the second edition of his *Language, Truth and Logic* Ayer writes that even if the principle of verification is invalid, yet his views on morality (statements of ethics) would be the same, because "in fact, I believe this analysis to be valid on its own account."[45]

Critical Reflections

G.E. Moore in his most authoritative and convincing work *Principia Ethica* castigates those who consider the ethical terms such as "good," "bad," "vice," "virtue" as natural properties of the objects. For he considers that the term "good" is indefinable, inasmuch as it is unanalysable. Like the term "yellow," holds Moore, "good" is a simple notion. Simples cannot be analysed into further simples otherwise they are not simples at all. Moore

43. A.J. Ayer, op. cit., p. 246.

44. A.J. Ayer, "His Not Reason Why?" interview with Miriam Gross, *Observer* (London), 24 February 1980.

45. A.J. Ayer, *Language, Truth and Logic*, p. 27.

says: ". . . if I am asked 'what is good?' my answer is that 'good is good', and that is the end of the matter. Or if I am asked 'How is good to be defined?' my answer is that 'it cannot be defined', and that is all I have to say about it."[46]

What Moore wants to convey is that complexes alone can be analysed into various simples. For example, argues Moore, "horse" as a complex notion can be defined (every definition involves description of the object in question), since a horse has many properties and qualities. But every quality or property by itself is not definable as it is a simple unit. In other words, "they are simply something which you think of or perceive, and to anyone who cannot think of or perceive them, you can never by any definition, make their nature known."[47] In that case good as a quality must either be thought of or perceived. But it sounds odd to say that "good" can be perceived. The natural properties of objects like, colour, taste, smell, etc. can be perceived but good is not a natural property of anything. Hence it cannot be perceived. According to Moore, this is the problem faced by many naturalists. The identification of good with any natural property leads us to "naturalistic fallacy." This fallacy, on Moore's view, has two important features — (1) to reduce non-natural properties to natural ones, and (2) an attempt to define indefinables.

Moore supposes that the quality of "good" is an intrinsic quality. However imperceptible a quality is, it is understood by the person who uses that term. People tend to interpret "good" in terms of pleasure which is desirable. Thus the term "good" has a definite meaning in moral science. The same analysis can be extended to the term "beauty" in aesthetics. Like "good" the term "beauty" is indefinable. Still we tend to

46. G.E. Moore, "The Indefinability of Good", in *Readings in Twentieth Century Philosophy*, ed. W.P. Alston and G. Nakhnikian, p. 235.

47. Ibid.

use that term whenever we have an aesthetic sense of appreciation of an object or situation in question. Like Moore, Ayer too opposes ethical naturalism. But, Moore does not reduce ethical concepts to mere emotions of the speaker whereas Ayer does.

It is important here to explain emotivism as advocated by C.L. Stevenson and J.O. Urmson. Though there are certain similarities of interpretation between Ayer and these two philosophers, the latter's interpretation of emotivism does not have much negative impact on ethical judgements. The theories put forward by these two thinkers are worth consideration.

Stevenson believes that all the ethical questions can be reduced to the form "is so and so good." He sets out two important tasks in order to clarify ethical questions. First of all, one must be able to distinguish whether something is "good" or not. Secondly, "goodness" must consist of certain magnetic force. In other words, it must evoke a sense of responsibility to act in favour of it. These two conditions, on Stevenson's account can be fulfilled provided "goodness" in a thing is not to be verified by the use of any scientific method. If these conditions are acceptable, holds Stevenson, the emotive theory recognises that the significance of ethical judgements is to promote a kind of interest in the individual. All the traditional theories provided us with descriptive analysis of ethical pronouncements. Such an analysis was not at all fruitful in analysing the nature of the term "good." In an attempt to provide a clear-cut analysis of ethical judgements, Stevenson distinguishes descriptive use of any term from its dynamic use. The dynamic use of the term gives us exact causal or dispositional property of the term in question. Thus every emotive meaning is associated with its dynamic use of the term but not with its descriptive use.[48] The meaning of "good" is

48. C.L. Stevenson, "The Emotive Meaning of Ethical Terms", *Mind*, vol. XLVII, 1937, p. 45.

derived from its magnetic force. In short, an emotive meaning is the outcome of the dynamic use of a term. In this way, what Stevenson expresses is that emotive meaning is not devoid of any meaning, instead it renders all ethical pronouncements meaningful irrespective of their fulfilling the criterion of verification.

On the other hand, Urmson tries to interpret the term "good" in terms of "grading" without committing himself to naturalism or non-naturalism. His analysis is as follows. Grading of a class of things is an activity of physical or mental nature. For example, a fruit vendor grades, say, bananas into fine, good, fairly good and moderate categories. While doing so, according to Urmson, the fruit vendor must take care of two important things: (1) what does he mean by grading? and (2) what are the properties or qualities that are taken into account to grade a thing as fine, good, fairly good and moderate? Here the application of a definite grading label to a thing reveals that a thing possesses an extra property apart from the properties that it shares with other things that belong to the same class. This extra or unique property is neither a natural one nor derived through intuition. This unique property which helped a fruit vendor to place a thing in a particular gradation is something like the term "good" that we use in ethics. A fruit vendor may not be able to explain how this gradation is done though he knows the criteria of gradation. Similarly, a moralist would not be able to explain in concrete terms what he means by good and the criteria to judge goodness.[49]

To sum up, Ayer's approach towards ethical pronouncements is totally negative. Unequivocally, we cannot verify moral statements in the sense in which we can verify the statements of natural science. But morality is a social

49. J.O. Urmson, "On Grading", *Mind* (London), vol. LIX, 1950.

relationship and a special form of social consciousness. Instead of an objective investigation of categories of ethics, Ayer seeks to elucidate how certain moral attributes are used. Moral attributes are social characteristics of actions and are determined by social import of actions. Later, Wittgenstein rightly held that the language of ethics has its own significance, and moral discourse must be treated in a manner different from other discourses. In fact, the thinkers like R.M. Hae, R.L. Stevenson, Stephen Toulmin and P.H. Nowell-Smith offered different types of paradigm for the analysis of moral language. Furthermore, they all agreed that normative judgements are outside the purview of logical or linguistic analysis. They can only be analysed in terms of social relations existing in a society. In fact, the principle of verification, the meaning of a statement is the method or mode of its verification in experience, painstakingly explains the nature of reality in terms of sensory perceptions.

5

The Nature of Perception

We have discussed how the principle of verification in any attempted amendment rests upon the possibility of having a certain sort of sensory experience. Now the problem before Ayer is how to construct such an experience in terms of sensations. Thus the principle of verification is connected with the nature of perception in logical positivism. Perception has been regarded as one of the important sources of knowledge. It is by means of perception that our sense organs come into contact with the objects of the external world. Before going to make any attempt to analyse the nature of perception as proposed by Ayer, it would be necessary, here, to highlight the problems related to perception as a source of knowledge.

What is Perception?

It is generally regarded that perception is a process that involves conscious activity of sensory experience. In other words, perception involves sensation and the interpretation of the sense-given contents. As pointed out by Immanuel Kant, pure sense-experience (material element) without proper interpretation (formal element) cannot qualify itself as knowledge of reality. Sense-experience is a process where the external objects affect the sense organs in various ways. This results in the identification of an object external to us. But it is the interpretation of the effects of objects on senses that makes the perceptual activity complete. Unlike Kant, empiricists conceive that mere sensation or reflection can be regarded as perception. Whatever is given in sensation, according to empiricists, is direct, hence it is true. The difference between Kant and empiricists lies in their interpretation of the concept "experience." According to Kant, experience is an admixture of material (sense given) and formal (conscious activity of mind) elements, while empiricists restricted the term "experience" to mere sensory experience. The problem of interpretation of perception as a process is as old as philosophy. The generations of philosophers have tried their level best to explain away the problem of perception by suggesting the various alternatives of interpretation. In spite of their strenuous efforts to solve the problem, it still remains as a vexed problem of epistemology.

In line with their empiricist predecessors, logical positivists argue that our knowledge of any object is based on immediate data supplied by our sensory experience. They pose the questions such as: What is it that we really perceive when, as we normally say, we perceive physical objects? Are the objects we perceive real? Do we have any valid grounds for believing in the existence of the world outside us? Ayer envisages that the problem of perception has been directed to give an account of relationship of sense-experience to physical objects. It has been regarded by the analysts that the relationship between sense-experience and physical objects is only logical, but not causal, i.e. a matter of showing how our statements about physical objects like chairs, tables can be shown to be equivalent to the statements about sensory experiences. Ayer argues that we can have only a direct, certain, and uninferred acquaintance with our sense-experience; with our sense-contents or sense-data. Consequently, if our beliefs about objects are to have any secure foundation, they must consist in what we directly are aware of, viz. sense-data. Ayer claims that the main purpose of introducing "sense-datum" language is to uphold phenomenalism as a theory of perception. According to this linguistic phenomenalism, the statements about physical objects can be translated into statements about sense-data without any residue. Like Humean sense-impressions, these sense-data are regarded as transitory, discrete, unconnected elements of sense-experience. The so-called logical relationship between sensory experience and physical objects reduces physical objects to the level of "logical constructs." Ayer advocates this form of phenomenalism (linguistic phenomenalism) in his *Language, Truth and Logic*, and *The Foundations of Empirical Knowledge*. But he disowns this position in his later work, *The Problem of Knowledge*. Nevertheless, his position on sense-data remains the same. It is the philosophy of David Hume which Ayer moulded into his own logical framework.

What are Sense-data?

The term "sense-datum" has been used by philosophers in different senses. In spite of the subtle differences that one finds in the usage of the term "sense-datum," the main contention in introducing the language of sense-datum is to show that in perception what we immediately know is a sense-datum but not a physical object. Bertrand Russell has introduced the term "sense-data" in his book, *The Problems of Philosophy* (1912), in connection with "appearance and reality" where he writes as follows:

> Let us give a name "sense-data" to the things that are immediately known in sensations, such as colours, sounds, smells, hardnesses, roughnesses, and so on. We shall give the name sensation to the experience of being immediately aware of these things.[1]

Russell gives the name sense-data to the object of sensation that are directly given in sense-experience. Following Russell's line of argument, David Pears interprets "sense-datum" in the

1. Bertrand Russell, *The Problems of Philosophy* (London, 1912), p. 17.

following way: "The common factor in its meaning is 'what is given by senses'; which is contrasted with 'what is inferred.' "[2] These philosophers interpreted sense-datum in a way that what is given by senses might be how things look to us, or how they sound to us, etc.

G.E. Moore, another advocate of sense-datum theory, gives the following explanation for the introduction of sense-data:

> I shall always talk of sense-data, when what I mean such things as this colour and size and shape or the patch which is of this colour and size and shape which I actually see. And when I want to talk of my seeing of them, I shall expressly call this seeing of "sense-data"; or, if I want a term which will apply equally to all these senses.[3]

According to Moore, all the qualities (sensible qualities) of objects have power to produce sense-data in us. These sense-data are directly apprehended in sense-perception. Further Moore holds that sense-data of one person cannot be shared by any other person. In that way they are private to one's own self.

H.H. Price, who has been regarded as the guardian of "sense-data," holds that one can doubt the existence of anything except sense-data. He argues:

> I can doubt whether there is any material thing at all, perhaps what I took for a tomato was really a reflection; perhaps I am even the victim of some hallucination. One thing however I cannot doubt; that there exists a red patch of a round and somewhat bulgy shape standing out from a background of other colour patches, and having certain visual depths and

---

2. David Pears, *Bertrand Russell and British Tradition in Philosophy* (London, 1972), 2nd edn., p. 32.
3. G.E. Moore, *Some Main Problems of Philosophy* (New York, 1966), p. 45.

> that this whole field of colour is directly present to my consciousness, and says, This peculiar and ultimate manner of being presented to consciousness is called being given and that which is thus present is called a datum.[4]

The outcome of this observation is that whenever we see an object in question, there is a possibility that one can doubt the existence of that object but the only thing, claims Price, which cannot be doubted is the data given to the senses. What he calls this "given" is sense-data.

Having satisfied with the explanation given by sense-datum theorists why they have introduced sense-datum language, Ayer asserts that only "sense-data" are directly given in sense-experience. According to Ayer, sense-data are not the objects that are directly given in sense-perception but all those objects that are directly given in sense-perception are called sense-data.[5] This is in no way different from Humean conception. Hume holds the view that sense-impressions are not caused by objects, because, for Hume, a physical object is a bundle of sense-impressions. Like Hume, Ayer too reduces physical objects to sense-data. In agreement with other sense-datum theorists, Ayer says:

> . . . there is a general agreement among the philosophers who make use of the term "sense-datum" or some equivalent term, that what we immediately experience is always a sense-datum and never a material thing.[6]

Ayer maintains that the properties of sense-data, and their relation to material objects is to be solved by making it clear as to how the term "sense-datum" is to be used. For he considers

4. H.H. Price, *Perception* (London, 1961), p. 3.

5. A.J. Ayer, *The Foundations of Empirical Knowledge* (London, 1971), p. 59.

6. Ibid., p. 5.

that these are questions of logical nature but not empirical. Like any other sense-datum philosopher, Ayer argues that the nature of material objects is inferred from sense-data.[7] If sense-data are the only elements given in sense-experience, then nothing but sense-data alone exist. The question of existence and properties of physical objects does not arise since we do not know what they are. We cannot even be familiar with such a concept, since it is never given in sense-experience.[8] Then the physical objects, according to Ayer, are as fictitious as unicorns. In fact, Ayer arrives at this unpalatable conclusion by putting forward the argument from illusion.

The Argument from Illusion

In support of his earlier arguments in favour of sense-data, Ayer introduces the "argument from illusion" to show nothing but sense-data are directly given in sense-perception. Ayer contends that the principal point of this argument is that appearances of objects vary from one observer to the other, or the objects appear differently to the same observer under different conditions. He holds that the causes of these "delusive" appearances to a certain extent are determined by the state or conditions or factors such as intensity of light, the vantage point of the observer or the psychological state of observer, etc. For example, says Ayer, a coin that looks round from one angle may look elliptical from the other. Similarly, a stick which normally appears to be straight may appear to be bent when it is half submerged in the water. Therefore, one of the visual appearances of the coin is "delusive," since a coin cannot be both round and elliptical. Likewise, one of the visual appearances of the stick is "delusive," because it cannot be both straight and bent. In these cases, argues Ayer, what we see is not a real quality of a thing in question but something else.

---

7. A.J. Ayer, *The Foundations of Empirical Knowledge*, p. 2.
8. Ibid., p. 11.

This something else must be given a name and "it is for this purpose that philosophers have recourse to the term "sense-datum."[9] Ayer's main purpose in introducing this "argument from illusion" is to abolish the distinction between what appears to be the case and what is the case otherwise. Following the flag of H.H. Price, Ayer asserts that there is no intrinsic difference between perceptions which are "veridical" and those that are "delusive" since all that we immediately know is a sense-datum. To quote Ayer's remarks on this point:

> For it sometimes happens that a delusive experience is not only qualitatively indistinguishable from one that is veridical but it is also itself believed to be veridical, as in the example of a mirage; and, conversely, there are cases in which experiences that are actually veridical are believed to be delusive, as when we see something so strange or unexpected that we say to ourselves that we must be dreaming.[10]

From Ayer's point of view the distinction between veridical and delusive appearance of an object does not arise as we have direct acquaintance with sense-data, but not with the object. Unless one knows the real shape of the object one cannot judge the "veridical shape" of the object from its "delusive shape." Since physical objects are not given in sense-experience, we do not have any chance to know the real shape of an object excepting its immediate sense-data.

Trying to make a distinction between material objects and sense-data, Ayer writes:

> It is held to be characteristic of material things that their existence and their essential properties are independent of any particular observer . . . whether they are observed by one person or another, or not observed at all. But this, it is argued,

9. A.J. Ayer, *The Foundations of Empirical Knowledge*, p. 4.
10. Ibid., p. 7.

> has been shown not to be true of those objects that we immediately experience. And so the conclusion is reached that what we immediately experience is in no way a material thing.[11]

From the above statement of Ayer we can deduce that if only objects of sense-experience are sense-data, then, we cannot, strictly speaking, go beyond sense-data. Thus sense-data stand between the perceiver and the object as an iron curtain. Above all, if all that is known are sense-data then the question of existence of material objects does not arise. This position of Ayer is similar to that of Hume. For Hume, all that exist are sense-impressions. Like Hume, Ayer asserts that all that exist are sense-data. It is nothing but pure sensationalism.

Sense-datum Language

After providing the exposition of the argument from illusion, Ayer maintains, the question before us is to consider the validity of this argument, i.e. whether to consider the question that the nature of the objects that we immediately perceive is a linguistic one or as a matter of fact. Ayer opines that most of the philosophers consider it as a question of empirical nature. This apparently leads them to the conclusion that it is linguistically inconvenient and at the same time it is fallacious that we ever directly perceive a material thing. To avoid such unpalatable conclusions, claims Ayer, the question of validity concerning the argument from illusion should not be considered as an empirical one. According to Ayer, it is purely a question of linguistic nature. In support of his view, Ayer holds that no observations could settle the dispute between the philosophers[12] who advocate the view that material objects are

11. A.J. Ayer, op. cit., pp. 10-11.
12. Here Ayer is actually referring to naïve realist thesis, according to which everything that we perceive is part of the surface of a material object.

directly given in sense-experience and exponents of sense-datum theory. Sense-datum theorists maintain that the changes that take place in our perceptions of objects and the divergencies between the perceptions of different observers cannot be reconciled with the view that we directly perceive material objects. On the contrary, the opponents of this theory can always say that sense-datum theorists have too narrow a conception of material objects. Now the question at issue, claims Ayer, is about the choice of different languages. That is to say, we can talk sensibly and consistently about the nature of perception either in the sense-datum language or in material object language. It is left to the analysts to decide which language is most convenient.[13] As we have observed Ayer's preference is for sense-datum language.

People make suitable assumptions regarding the nature and behaviour of material objects. These assumptions, conceives Ayer, should not be considered as factual. The analysis of sensory contents (sense-data) and their relationship to physical objects is a logical one. Ayer ascribes a special meaning to the term "material thing" which is different from the ordinary use of it. We are very flexible in our ordinary use of terms. Whenever we see or touch an object, we believe that it really exists and feel that what we directly perceive is always a material thing. This belief is the product of misunderstanding of the word "perceive." Ayer uses the word "perceive" in an altogether different sense. For he considers that to perceive any object does not result in its existence.[14] However, says Ayer, the term "perceive" is also used in a sense that whatever is perceived does really exist. The difficulty in using this sense of the term "perceive" is that when a person undergoes an illusion of double vision by saying "I perceived two pieces of paper but there was really one piece there," then one has to accept

13. A.J. Ayer, *The Foundations of Empirical Knowledge* (London, 1971), pp. 17-18.

14. Ibid., pp. 19-21.

the version that both the pieces of paper exist, according to this usage, though there is one paper. In this sense, the term "perceive" is not applicable to expressions that are existentially delusive. Ayer argues that there would not be any problem so long as we keep the two usages of the term "perceive" distinct. Similarly, the term "see" also has the same implications just as the term "perceive." The important point to notice here is that we do not need both the usage in order to describe our perceptual experiences. Ayer claims that in order to avoid these difficulties the philosophers who introduced sense-datum theory have decided to use the terms "perceive" and "see" in a sense that what is seen or otherwise sensibly experienced must really exist and must have qualities that it appears to have is to designate modes of perception to delusive as well as veridical experiences. This kind of usage leads them to introduce sense-datum language. Ayer maintains that in the process of perceptual analysis, i.e. the relationship between our sense-experience and material things, since there is no qualitative distinction between "delusive" and "veridical" experiences, the terminology of sense-data can be applied to both the cases. The introduction of sense-data can be accepted as a rule of language in order to arrive at the conclusion that in all the cases of perception what we immediately know are "sense-data" but not material things.[15]

As a matter of fact, this is an example to show that logical positivists have taken refuge in scholastic and word-mongering. One may define words however one likes, but the question remains as to whether your words bear any relationship to real things. This is precisely meant to create confusion.

Arguments against Naïve Realism

Finally, the argument from illusion is directed against naïve

15. A.J. Ayer, *The Foundations of Empirical Knowledge*, p. 46.

realist thesis, according to which everything that we perceive is part of the surface of a material thing. Referring to H.H. Price's arguments against the naïve realist thesis of perception, Ayer holds:

> According to him, what is to be understood by Naïve Realism is the thesis that visual and actual sense-data are parts of the surfaces of material things; which, since he defines a sense-datum as that which is immediately given in perception, is equivalent to the thesis that it is always a material thing that we see or touch. And he maintains that if the argument from illusion proves nothing else, it does atleast refute this thesis.[16]

Ayer banks upon Price's arguments to refute naïve realism. He argues if a naïve realist uses the terms "see" and "touch" in a way that whatever is seen or touched does not mean that it exists or it does have properties that it appears to have, then we cannot disprove naïve realism on the basis of argument from illusion. But, if a naïve realist uses the term in any way other than the above-mentioned way then the argument will refute the thesis. According to Ayer, naïve realists take it for granted that whatever is seen or touched really exists.

Ayer interprets naïve realism in the following way: what a naïve realist states is "A is perceiving X where X refers to a material thing, can be analysed into A is sensing a sense-datum and knowing it to be part of the surface of X."[17] Ayer maintains that this argument can be refuted on the ground that naïve realist is saying that perceiving a material object can be analysed into sensing a sense-datum and knowing that it is part of the surface of the material object. But how can it be possible for a sense-datum by means of which A perceives a round coin, and the sense-datum by means of which B perceives the same coin as elliptical? This is self-contradictory, since a coin cannot be

16. A.J. Ayer, op. cit., p. 46

17. Ibid., p. 47.

both round and elliptical. Thus Ayer claims to have succeeded in his attempt to disprove naïve realism. It is also inconsistent with the conventions of sense-datum vocabulary. Trying to justify that his denial of naïve realism as a valid thesis of perception is not factual but only on linguistic grounds, Ayer remarks:

> . . . these so-called theories of perception are not theories at all in ordinary sense, and therefore that the notions of truth and falsehood, which we apply to scientific theories, are not applicable to them.[18]

Then the main object of analysis of perception is to recommend a suitable terminology which will enable us to explain the relation between material objects and the contents of sensory experience. This has become one of the most important preoccupations of logical positivists. If what Ayer says were true, viz. the notions of truth and falsity cannot be attributed to the contents of sensory experience, then the entire activity of analysing the contents of sensory experience becomes a futile exercise. In other words, it is an activity without any sense. Ayer's exposition of the nature of perception makes it clear that the doctrines of logical positivism, however disguised by logical phraseology, are parts of subjective idealism which, in the final analysis, reduce physical objects to one's own sensory contents. Ayer could not declare openly that physical objects are fictitious entities. He took refuge in linguistic phraseology to dismiss the view that physical objects exist independent of human consciousness.

Phenomenalism

Ayer's main contention in introducing sense-datum language is not only to disprove naïve realist thesis but also to uphold phenomenalism as a valid theory of perception. According to

18. A.J. Ayer, op. cit., p. 48.

phenomenalist theory, physical objects are reduced to atomic sense-experiences (sense-data). Ayer keeps on claiming that his approach towards this kind of reductionism is more logical rather than empirical. Thus he converts Humean phenomenalism (pure sensationalism) into linguistic phenomenalism, according to which the statements about physical objects can be translated into statements about sense-data. To record Ayer's statements on this point:

> We know that it must be possible to define material things in terms of sense-contents, because it is only by the occurrence of certain sense contents that the existence of any material thing can ever be in the least sense verified. And thus we see that we have not to inquire whether a phenomenalist theory of perception or some other sort of theory is correct but only what form of phenomenalist theory is correct.[19]

According to Ayer, the existence of material objects is dependent on the occurrences of certain sense-contents or sense-data. Moreover, Ayer took it for granted that phenomenalism is a valid theory of perception. His only problem, it seems, is: what form of phenomenalism is valid?

Ayer argues that the term "material thing" is not equivalent to any term or set of terms that stand for a species of sense-data. This is to say that any situation that confirms the existence of material thing must also confirm the existence of sense-data. This is because the sense-datum language is coined in such a way that in perception whenever it is true that we perceived a material thing it must also be true that a sense-datum is sensed.[20] Ayer states that the existence of a sense-datum in a given situation can be conclusively verified but it is not the case with material objects. Further, Ayer postulates that

---

19. A.J. Ayer, *Language, Truth and Logic*, p. 71.

20. A.J. Ayer, *The Foundation of Empirical Knowledge*, pp. 229-30.

whatever may be the situation, it is logically compatible with the hypothesis that the material thing cannot be in all respects what it appears to be, or it may not exist at all. Any other evidence may either weaken or support this hypothesis. But that will always result in the occurrence of further sense-data. Ayer emphasises that in fact there is nothing excepting the rule that the expression "sense-datum" is to be used to stand for whatever is, as a matter of fact, observed. He opines:

> Since it is impossible by any valid process or inference, to make a transition from what is observed to anything that is convinced as being, in principle, unobservable, all that the evidence in question will be evidence for, or against is the possible occurrence of further sense-data still.[21]

It implies that from observable evidence we can deduce anything unobservable, but it is possible through the medium of further sense-data. Thus Ayer declares that the term "material thing" is not equivalent to any term or group of terms that refer to sense-data. Based on the above argument, Ayer concludes that any proposition that refers to a material thing must somehow be expressed in terms of "sense-data." In short, it is to say "that material things are nothing but collections of actual and possible sense-data."[22] This shows that the categorical statements of material objects are reducible to the hypothetical statements of sense-data. From this definition Ayer draws "the formal consequence" that material things are constituted by sense-data. This conclusion is unassailable, holds Ayer, because it is a formal consequence of the definition. A material thing by definition is a logical construct out of actual and possible sense-data.

To sum up, the phenomenalistic position is that no

21. A.J. Ayer, *The Foundation of Empirical Knowledge*, p. 231.
22. Ibid.

knowledge of material objects is possible, all or only knowledge of sense-experience (sense-data) is possible, and such knowledge is direct, certain and basic. In more linguistic terms no statements about material objects are basic. The only basic propositions are the propositions that describe our immediate sensory experiences (sense-data). This thesis of phenomenalism came to be criticised by Isaiah Berlin. Berlin's main objection is that phenomenalism makes "actualities depend upon possibilities" and that it has the consequence that any analysis of a material object statement would be infinitely long and therefore it cannot be carried out even in principle. Berlin argues that the statements about material objects are "categorical," whereas the statements about sense-data are "hypothetical." Then how is it logically possible to reduce the categorical statements about material objects to the statements about sense-data. Berlin writes:

> A categorical existential material object sentence, as "the table is next door," or "there is a table next door," is used at the very least to describe something which is occurring or being characterised at the time of speaking . . . , and being characterised or occurring, unless the contrary is specifically stated or implied not intermittently but continuously, and in any case not "hypothetically is a very artificial and misleading way of saying, that it is not in the ordinary sense, occurring at all. . . ."[23]

According to Berlin, the phenomenalistic analysis of unperceived material objects in terms of sense-data will result in a series of hypothetical statements. But a material object statement describes the properties that are existing in the material object consequently categorical. Logically, Berlin shows, a categorical statement cannot be equivalent to a series

---

23. Isaiah Berlin, "Empirical Propositions and Hypothetical Statements", *Mind* (London), N.S., vol. LIX, no. 59, 1950, p. 235.

of hypothetical statements. Thus he concludes that phenomenalistic analysis of material object statements cannot be carried out.

Ayer, who was once an adherent of phenomenalism, has gradually deviated from this position. In his work *The Problem of Knowledge*, Ayer holds that reduction of material object statements into sense-datum statements is not possible because no finite number of sense-datum statements can ever be equivalent to a material object statement, since the numbers of possible appearances which object may manifest are unlimited.[24] In spite of this problem, logical positivists are complacent with their success in introducing sense-datum language. Whether reductionism is a fruitful enterprise or not, the fact remains that what we immediately perceive in sense-experience are sense-data but not material objects. Thus Ayer's position on sense-data remains the same.

Critical Reflections

Maurice Cornforth[25] feels that the assumption behind the argument from illusion is that in order to have knowledge of the reality we start from those things (sense-data) which are essentially private, and move from them to the knowledge of public world. It is an obvious problem how this result can be achieved. Any adequate understanding of sense-experience must involve an understanding of how this is possible. And this implies in turn an account of the concept of perception which takes perception to be based on certain basic experiences (sense-experiences). In those experiences we are provided with knowledge of certain immediate entities (sense-data) on which our knowledge of physical objects is dependent. If the objects

---

24. A.J. Ayer, *The Problem of Knowledge*, p. 124.
25. Maurice Cornforth, "Is Analysis a Useful Method in Philosophy?" *Aristotelian Society Supplement* (London, 1934), pp. 92-95.

of those perceptions are sense-data, then these sense-data are more basic than the physical objects with which they are contrasted. Thus, the position of Ayer involves both ontological and epistemological claims of sense-data. From the standpoint of ontology, it is sense-data which are supposed to be the ultimate constituents of reality, and from the standpoint of epistemology sense-data are the basic objects of knowledge.

Anthony Quinton's arguments are directed against the view that the statements about sense-data are basic, since they are directly given in sense-experience, while the statements about the material objects are inferred or constructed from sense-datum statements. He argues that to describe a material object statement to be certain is largely dependent upon the conditions in which it is presented to our minds and what is known about it. The familiarity and stability, maintains Quinton, of an object is determined by the question whether a description of that particular experience is certain or not. Thus, he arrives at the conclusion that one cannot be said to perceive anything unless one is in a position to describe it. Nevertheless, contends Quinton, one may commit a mistake in describing a particular experience because of loose correlation of language and on account of unfavourable conditions of observation. But this source of mistake does not substantiate a theory of acquaintance and to show one category is logically superior to another.[26]

Further Quinton argues that the relation between physical objects and sensory experience of those objects in question is not logical but causal. He holds:

> Our beliefs about objects are based on experience in a way that requires not justification but explanation. Experiences are not my reasons for my beliefs about objects — to have an

26. Anthony Quinton, "The Problem of Perception", in *The Philosophy of Perception,* ed. G.J. Warnock (Oxford, 1977), pp. 76-78.

> experience is to know or to believe anything which could be a reason in this sense — though they may be the reasons for my believing what I do from the point of view of a psychologist.[27]

Quinton's arguments are very sensible. It is true that our justification of the existence of objects external to us is not solely dependent on the sensory experiences. As envisaged by Quinton, the doctrines concerning acquaintance and basic statements are the outcome of a search for standard perceptual conditions, but no standard perceptual conditions are perfect and there is no reason to say that a particular experience is basic and other is not.

Austin and Ryle are also too critical of sense-datum language. Both of them attack sense-datum language from the standpoint of ordinary language philosophy.

Austin's criticism is basically intended to disprove the doctrines of A.J. Ayer and H.H. Price. Austin in his work *Sense and Sensibilia* (1962) relentlessly argues the view that what we "directly" perceive are sense-data but not material things. People hold such assumptions, says Austin, since they are fascinated by certain words or facts which have not been carefully studied, understood or described. The terms used in explaining these facts or situations are far more vague and subtle than the exponents of these views thought of. A wider range of examples would disabuse us of the view that things must be the way sense-datum philosophers say they are. For that matter naïve realism, supposes Austin, is also a superficial theory. Austin expresses the feeling:

> One of the most important points to grasp is that these two terms, sense-data and material thing live by taking in each

---

27. A.J. Ayer, op. cit., p. 83.

> other's washing; what is spurious is not one term of the pair, but the antithesis itself.[28]

The problem, as pointed out by Austin, is very much rooted in the so-called antithesis between sense-data and material objects. It is a mistake to think that we always perceive one thing or the other but so many things. Austin says that sense-datum philosophers first set up the stage for sense-data by arguing that ordinary man would say that he perceives material things. But, according to Austin, this is not true, because common man does not normally use the term "material object" for the objects that he perceives in his day-to-day life. . . . Suppose the term "material object" covers a wide range of objects such as tables, chairs, cats and rocks, then the "ordinary man" under the heading "things he perceived" includes things like "People's voices, rivers, mountains, flames, rainbows, pictures on the screen at the cinema, pictures in books or hung on walls, vapour gases. . . ."[29] But these are certainly not material objects. The first step towards sense-datum fold is taken when one claims that there is one and only one sort of thing that one can perceive, because if one thinks that he has perceived something but not a material object, then he thinks his senses deceived him. Further, the descriptions of one's sensory occurrences lead one to think that one is not perceiving a material object, but only a sense-datum. Austin says this is all nonsense. He argues that if one sees non-material objects like rainbows, then how does a material one look like? The ships which appear nearer than they actually are? In all these cases, does anyone think that his senses deceived him?

Austin does not accept the view that ordinary man's belief in the existence of material objects needs justification in every case. If a person is more sensible and reflective he would

---

28. J.L. Austin, *Sense and Sensibilia* (Oxford, 1962), p. 4.

29. Ibid., p. 8.

definitely think that all the cases of perception of material objects need not be justified. But a sense-datum philosopher does not even see this much. Suppose one doubts what he sees, then he gets enough certainty from the perceptual world for practical purposes, but he may not be absolutely certain about it. According to Austin, a sense-datum philosopher not only disallows the view that we can perceive material objects directly but also is prepared to distrust our own senses. He sticks to his view that what we always perceive is a sense-datum but not a material object. In this way, the sense-datum theorist's doubt is not a just little doubt in borderline cases, but a doubt that cannot be cleared.

Further, Austin says that the sense-datum philosopher introduces the notion of sense-data which stand between the perceiver and what is "out there," and which pass us the information about the outside world. In other words, these sense-data act as television broadcast between the studio and the man's living room. Here the layman along with the philosopher is enclosed in the room. The only way he can find out what is going on outside is to watch the television set. The layman does not have any direct accessibility to the real happening of the world outside us. With regard to the genuineness of the telecast, philosopher is always there to tell him whether the transmission is imperfect.[30] This is to say that one is half way through the sense-datum abyss, one wonders how often one is going to be deceived by his senses. But, holds Austin, one does not say that he is often deceived by his senses as conceived by a sense-datum philosopher. Even if one is deceived by his senses in certain cases, this deception is attributed to many factors such as: (a) the person's deranged sense organs; (b) the abnormal conditions of perception, and (c) where a wrong inference is made from what one perceives, etc.

30. J.L. Austin, *Sense and Sensibilia,* pp. 10-12.

Austin's next target of attack is the argument from illusion.[31] This argument is introduced with a view to convincing people to accept sense-data as what they perceive under abnormal conditions. It is then argued that the same thing happens even under normal conditions. Austin draws this argument from Ayer. It is shown in the exposition of the argument from illusion, that different observers see material objects differently on the same occasion, and on successive occasions the same observer sees changes in the object which could not. Hence, what they are seeing is not a material object, but appearances of its sense-data. The straight stick partly immersed in the water looks bent. But stick could not have changed its shape. Hence, we are seeing a bent sense-datum of the stick. In some versions of the argument it is also said that in the illusory perception what we perceive cannot be a feature of a material object. This leads us to believe that there is no phenomenological difference between illusory and veridical experiences. Consequently, there are no reasons for saying that in the case of a veridical experience what we perceive is a feature of a material object in question. It is this point that is the main target of Austin's attack. Austin feels that the entire argument from illusion is trading on the confusion between "illusion" and "delusion." He differentiates illusion from delusion. Every elementary textbook on psychology, holds Austin, contains several examples of optical illusion. For example, several lines of same length shaded in different colours are made to look unequal in their length: two parallel lines are made to look as if they were crossing each other. Thus an illusion is a case of seeing something for something else. As pointed out by Austin, one can be on guard against illusions. But, delusion is a situation where we create something out of nothing. In the cases of delusion something is always conjured up. Hence we cannot

31. J.L. Austin, *Sense and Sensibilia*, pp. 20-24.

be on guard against delusions, since they are the products of mental disorder. Austin's analysis of illusions and delusions is a very sensible step to show that sense-datum philosophers are on a wrong footing.

Another weakness of the argument from illusion, according to Austin, is its insistence on normal and abnormal conditions. Austin questions, what does one mean by normal? How does one know that the distance between the object and the perceiver is a normal distance? What does one mean by normal light? What does one mean by normal view? Unless the sense-datum philosopher makes it clear as to how he is going to define the term "normal," it is impossible for one to distinguish normal from abnormal conditions. Austin is sure that he cannot make it clear. Similarly, what does sense-datum philosopher mean by direct? The term, according to Austin, has different interpretations. Like the term "normal," the term "direct" needs clarification from the standpoint of a sense-datum philosopher to distinguish direct from indirect. Unless and until the sense-datum philosopher makes it clear as to how he is going to interpret these terms, the argument from illusion is not considered as a valid argument at all.

Ryle questions the legitimacy of the use of the verbs like "see," "hear," and "taste" in speaking about sense-data. According to him, these verbs do not represent the sensations "neat." These verbs are only used in the talk about sensations. To quote Ryle:

> We ordinarily use these words for a special family of perceptions, namely, factual and kinaesthetic perceptions and perceptions of temperatures, as well as localisable pains and discomforts.[32]

When someone says that he has a burning or throbbing

32. Gilbert Ryle, *The Concept of Mind* (Harmondsworth, 1978), p. 191.

sensation we do not normally talk of this painful type of sensation as if it were existing apart from his feeling of it. But, when we talk about such a perception, asserts Ryle, we use sensation as a name for it, or use sensation to refer to one of the many aspects in the act of perceiving. We may be tempted to distinguish a sensation from what it is a sensation of. This leads us to create intermediatories between us and the world outside us. These intermediatories are named as sense-data.

Ryle holds that a person's pain stops when he stops feeling it. But, when he stops seeing horse races or tasting wines, the race goes on and the wine is still there. But something did really stop and a convenient name for it is a person's view or tasting. These sorts of things, claims Ryle, have been converted into sense-data and it is argued, whenever we say we see a material object we are really seeing a sense-datum. We no longer see things but only usual sensations. Further Ryle asserts: "I shall try to prove that this whole theory rests upon a logical howler, the howler, namely, of assimilating the concept of sensation to the concept of observation. . . ."[33]

Ryle puts forward a number of interesting arguments in defence of his assertion. The first one is the type of infinite regress argument which he uses against the view that intelligence consists in theorising. The argument is as follows:

Suppose, what a sense-datum theorist says is true, then having a visual sensation of a horse race involves sensing a patchwork of colour. So having a glimpse of a horse race is analysed into having a glimpse of what we see, namely, a patchwork of colour. But Ryle illustrates that if having a look or glimpse of "X" means you have no sensation, then having a look or glimpse of that sensation involves having another, call it "Y"; but having a look or glimpse of "Y" involves another,

33. Gilbert Ryle, *The Concept of Mind*, p. 203.

and there you go on to infinity. If each has a sensation, it involves in further observing or seeing of something then there is no end to this process of perceiving or sensing. For this reason Ryle argues that any attempt to justify what one observes in the world around us in terms of sense-data leads to infinite regress. As a matter of fact, for the information given in the sense-datum what one observes in sensing it will itself require justification.

Ryle points out, it is a contradiction to say that someone is observing something but having no sensation of it. Observations involve sensations. In an attempt to exemplify it, Ryle says: "If all the clothes are concatenations of stitches, absurdity results from saying that all stitches are themselves very tiny clothes."[34] He maintains that observing consists in having sensations, but sensations cannot be like observing. Thus, according to Ryle, to confuse observation of material objects with sensing sense-data is to commit a category mistake. Ryle holds that to say I observe sensations is like saying that I spell syllables because, "Syllables are not the sort of things which can be either correctly or incorrectly spelt."[35] Another salient feature of Ryle's attack on sense-datum theorists is his recognition of achievement words. For he considers that all the verbs of perceiving are "achievement words." The acts of perception are the accomplishments which require some degree of training, skill and effort.[36]

If the arguments given against sense-datum theory are sound enough, then there are no such things called sense-data. Every attempt to construct sense-data between the perceiver and the objects results in some problem or the other.

From the standpoint of science it is argued that the sensory knowledge is the reflection of reality through the sense organs:

---

34. Gilbert Ryle, *The Concept of Mind*, p. 204.
35. Ibid., p. 196.
36. Ibid., p. 226.

visual, auditory, tactile, olfactory, and gustatory. The sense-organs are the only channels through which information about the reality can penetrate into our consciousness. Any process of cognition, therefore, begins with impressions arising from the action of material objects on the sense organs. Sensory cognition is affected in three main forms: sensations, perceptions and representations.[37] Sensory cognition is important because it provides direct knowledge of the reality. The development of knowledge in all sciences begins with the direct perceptions, observation and description of objects and their properties. It is only on the basis of sense-perception that factual material is accumulated which forms the groundwork for theoretical generalisations that help to discover the natural laws.

Sensory knowledge proceeds from the premises that sensations and representations are the subjective image of the objective reality. This means that the source of sensations lies outside the subjective world of our consciousness. Sense-perceptions reflect properties of the objects in this phenomenal reality. Cognitive activity of sensations is manifested in the fact that an image, being a reflection, does not and cannot exist outside the perceiver's mind. Sensations are dependent in a defined way on the organism's state as a whole. For instance, honey tastes sour to a sick person. People perceive colours differently. This may be due to colour blindness. The subjectivity of our sensory-experiences does not, however, just refer to pathological cases. Our sensory images are subjective because they are not identical to things, their relationship and properties. For they are an ideal form of reality produced in

37. Sensations are the elementary results of the action of the objects on man's sense organs. Perceptions are the reflections of an object arising in the consciousness owing to the effect of the objects on the senses. Thus sensations are elements of perception.

our minds. Sense-datum philosophers, instead of giving a scientific analysis of nature of perception, always try to interpret perception in an abstract sense, which divorces knowledge from reality. They conceive that in all the cases of perception what we perceive is a sense-datum but not a material object. This they tried to prove from the so-called "argument from illusion." To give a scientific explanation of Ayer's argument from illusion, a straight stick looks bent when it is partly immersed in water because of various extraneous factors. The theory of refraction in physics explains that when a ray of light travels obliquely from one medium to another, it is refracted at the surface separating the two media. This refraction occurs because light travels in different velocities in different media. Sometimes it happens, exactly, that sensory information turns out to be erroneous because of the subjective character of perception. Through a visual error, for instance, we may take a rope for a snake or a mussel for a silver coin. It does not mean that we must always suspect our sensations and only assess them as a kind of hieroglyph.

Hence, in the first place, whether a stick looks bent in the water or not, it cannot be correct to suppose that the object of our sense perception is analysable into a collection of fleeting sense-data. These sense-data are purely metaphysical invention. They have no real existence, and have no place in any science. Having postulated such a mode of existence Ayer and other logical positivists proceeded to argue that since only sense-data are given in consciousness, therefore, causality and power of things to influence and change one another in this reality must be an illusion. But this argument must go the other way round. Since sense-data are entirely "inert" and powerless units of sensory-perception, they are considered to be fictitious entities.

The result of this discussion is that in perception what we know are properties of material objects in the form of subjective images. This lays foundation to the view that material objects exist independent of perceiving minds. Man's sensations contain that which really lies outside his perceptions. In this connection it is necessary to discuss the distinction between "appearance" and "reality." In fact, appearance and reality are the two important categories expressing different aspects of things, stages of knowledge, and different depths in understanding of an object. Knowledge of an object begins with the identification of its external properties and the relationship of objects in physical space. Getting to know their causal and profound law-governed relationships leads to the disclosure of essence (reality). The logic of the development of knowledge and the needs of social practice together compelled man to make a sharp distinction between how an object appears to us and what it actually is. External properties (appearances) of the objects are given in sense-perception, while the essences (internal nature of things) which some philosophers like Locke and Kant claim "unknown and unknowable" are knowable through man's practical experience. As rightly pointed out by Lenin:

> There is no difference in principle between the phenomena and the thing-in-itself, and there cannot be any such difference. The only difference is between what is known and what is not yet known. . . . In the theory of knowledge, as in every sphere of science, we must think dialectically, that is, we must not regard our knowledge as ready-made and unalterable, but must determine how knowledge emerges from ignorance, how incomplete inexact becomes more complete and more exact.[38]

Thus the real field of knowledge is not the given fact about the things as they are, but the critical evaluation of them in order to go beyond their given form. But for Ayer, there is no

38. V.I. Lenin, *Materialism and Empirio-Criticism* (Moscow, 1973), p. 90.

distinction between appearance and reality, since all that exist are sense-data. These sense-data are mere appearances of the phenomena. On Ayer's account, there is no chance for us to go behind these appearances (sense-data), since sense-data are regarded as the bedrocks of knowledge. Ayer's empiricist predecessor, David Hume said the same thing when he recognised sense-impressions to be the bedrocks of human knowledge.

This is the manner how Ayer claims to vindicate the reductive analysis by using principle of verification. All that is verifiable are nothing but sense-data. The sense-data of Ayer leave us nothing but shadows of the objects as in the myth of the cave of Plato, where all that the prisoners in the cave could see are the shadows on the wall of the cave of the outside world. Likewise, for Ayer sense-data are the ultimate constituents of reality. This is how Ayer arrives at his ontology through his epistemology.

6

The Problem of Induction

AYER'S theory of causation springs from his ontology. As has been pointed out in the preceding chapter, for Ayer all that really exist are sense-data. These sense-data are supposed to be the ultimate constituents of reality. In other words, they are of cardinal importance to construct a proper epistemological system. These fleeting, momentary, unconnected elements (sense-data) do not influence each other as the relations that exist among them are purely external but not internal relations. Above all, there is no continuity in them. What we suppose that continuity is nothing but temporal regularity that is given in sense-perception. The whole theory of causation of Ayer rests upon this very notion. It implies that there is no necessary connection between events that happen in this phenomenal world. On this account of causation the universal laws of Nature can be built by observing fleeting sense-data. This conception of Ayer leads us to the problem of induction. Since there is no necessary causal connection between one event and the other, excepting some temporal regularity in the phenomena, which is given in sense-experience, Ayer cannot solve the problem of induction with his ontological framework. The supposed problem of induction is: what justification do we have to give that instances that held good in the past are going to hold good in future? Thus, causation and induction are inseparable from each other. In this chapter, it has been tried to show that Ayer's position on causation and induction is not substantially different from that of Hume.

What is Causation?

Causation or causality is one of the most important categories of experience in philosophy as well as in science. It is believed that every happening in this phenomenal world is attributed to some cause. Similarly, it is assumed that similar causes produce similar effects under given conditions. Sometimes, it is viewed that multiple causes may give rise to one single effect, and one single cause may result in multiple effects. Philosophers and scientists have interpreted causation in different ways. Though the interpretations differ from philosopher to philosopher and scientist to scientist, the general feature of causation that has got universal assent is that cause always precedes the effect. In short, we can say that cause is an antecedent event that is always followed by a specific effect or a group of effects that is considered to be the consequent in definite spatio-temporal relations.

The philosophers of the antiquity had thought of causation as an essential feature of the explanation of reality. They have attributed the existence of this phenomenal world, and order and purpose of various events in this phenomenal world, to a first or a primordial cause. For instance, ancient Greek philosophers were in search of a first cause from which everything has emerged. Thales, who is regarded as the father of philosophy, conceived that water is the cause of everything. Subsequently, the philosophers like Anaximander, Anaximanes and Heraclitus interpreted the cause of everything in terms of "indeterminate stuff" "air" and "flux" and "fire" respectively. In Plato's philosophy, the eternal "Forms" or "Ideas" are the supposed causes of the world of objects. Perhaps, it was Aristotle for the first time in the history of philosophy who provided us with a fourfold theory of causation. Being a natural philosopher, Aristotle felt the importance of causation in explaining the nature of phenomena and various processes that take place in Nature. According to him, there are four important causes, namely, (1) formal cause, (2) material cause, (3) efficient cause, and (4) final cause. He illustrated his fourfold theory of causation in the following way. For example, a carpenter wants to make a teapoy out of a piece of wood. First of all, the carpenter must have an idea of the "form" of the teapoy. Thus formal cause is one of the preconditions for the teapoy to exist. Next, the carpenter selects a specific quality of wood to make a teapoy out of it. This becomes a material cause. The carpenter himself and the paraphernalia that he uses in chipping the wood to make a teapoy out of it are considered to be the efficient cause. The final form of the teapoy is the final cause. Strictly speaking, what Aristotle considered the causes are nothing but certain conditions required to make a teapoy. Apart from that, the supposed final cause is nothing but an effect of the first three causes. As a matter of fact, the first three causes are followed by a definite effect. In a genuine sense of the term "cause" the final cause is not a cause at all. Another flaw in Aristotle's theory is that Aristotle could not distinguish natural causation from the artificial one. The artificial causation is a man-made situation that is restricted to certain conditions. In the case of natural causation, the processes that take place in Nature are not arbitrary but are necessary and universal.

Coming to medieval thinkers, they have interpreted causation in terms of natural and supernatural. All the natural events that take place in this phenomenal world are mere effects of the supernatural causes. Especially, the theologians have made such inferences that God or some supernatural spirit is the cause of everything that is happening in this phenomenal world. What theologians do is that they proceed from knowable natural effects to unknowable supernatural first cause or causes. On the other hand, common sense theorists hold the view that both causes and effects are knowable. They argue that unless one knows the nature of the cause, one will not be able to say that particular causes give rise to particular effects.

Inferences are possible between two knowable events, but one cannot infer a knowable event from an unknowable one. However, the relation between two events may be intrinsic and necessary or mere temporal one. Those who endorse the view that the relation between two events is intrinsic and necessary are called determinists, while those who hold the view that the relation between two events is always temporal and sequential are called indeterminists. Now the entire problem of causation trades between these two contrasting viewpoints. Those who adhere to determinism claim that the so-called traditional problem of induction is a pseudo-problem. Contrary to this view, indeterminists say that we cannot give guarantee for those things which are in store for us. Thus they claim that the problem of induction is a genuine problem. This background will help us to understand the views expressed by Ayer with regard to causation and induction.

To start with Ayer's remarks on causation:

> Our view of the nature of causation remains substantially same as his (Hume's). And we agree with him that there can be no other justification for inductive reasoning than its success in practice. . . .[1]

According to Ayer, we do not have any valid grounds to justify induction, unless it is proved in sense-experience. Regarding the problem of induction Ayer writes that many philosophers have attempted to solve this problem of induction. However, the fact remains that it (the problem of induction) is very much in the same state where Hume left it. It appears that no inductive principle could ever be known a priori. At the same time, it is believed that any attempt to justify the inductive reasoning proves to be a futile attempt as it leads to circularity. It is also assumed that one inductive argument is used to justify the other

1. A.J. Ayer, *Language, Truth and Logic*, p. 74.

but there cannot be any general justification of induction. To this extent, holds Ayer, Hume is right in his perception of the problem of induction.[2]

It is obvious from the above argument of Ayer that Hume's influence on logical positivists in general is very strong. Humean psychological scepticism has been taken very seriously by Ayer and other logical positivists. As such scepticism and justification do not go together, especially with regard to empirical matters. Since the premises of both Hume and Ayer are the same, namely, pluralistic empiricism, their position on any other problem cannot be very different. Then, in order to understand Ayer's views on causality and induction, it is necessary to understand the central themes of Hume's theory. Alhough Hume's theory of causation has been outlined in the first chapter while discussing the development of empiricism, it would appear more appropriate to bring out the salient features of Humean theory in the present context.

Hume's View

Hume, who is supposed to have systematised empiricism, claims that all knowledge comes through sense-experience alone. He considers that reality is nothing but a stream of fleeting sensory impressions. Hume holds the position that to talk about objects is to refer to certain class of sense-impressions. Most of these impressions, for Hume, are not given in sense-experience simultaneously. Whatever is given in sense-experience can be restored in human mind in the form of memory, yet many slip from the mind. So to complete the whole picture of what we perceived, claims Hume, is possible only through possible impressions and these are possible through inference. Thus for Hume, all impressions that lead us beyond the present situation, except a few that depend on memory,

2. A.J. Ayer, R. Winch (eds.), *British Empirical Philosophers: Locke, Berkeley, Hume, Reid, J.S. Mill*, p. 26.

are based on the relation of cause and effect. This, Hume claims to be most important for the theory of knowledge.[3]

Hume's main intention is to show that there is no necessary causal connection between two contiguously existing impressions. What all that we see is some regularity that is given in sense-experience. As such there is no impression from which the idea of necessary connection is derived. Hume conceives that cause is temporally prior to the effect. A cause must be spatially and temporally contiguous to the effect. However, holds Hume, these two relations "contiguity" and "succession in time" alone are not sufficient. He observes:

> An object may be contiguous and prior to another, "without being considered as its cause. There is a necessary connection to be taken into consideration and that relation is of much greater importance, than any of the other two above mentioned.[4]

Though Hume recognises the importance of necessary connection, he rejects the idea of necessary connection on the ground that it is not given in sense-experience. Hume claims to explain away the necessary connection in the following way. He considers that it is not a logical connection, since every effect is entirely different from its cause. When two events are causally connected, says Hume, it is false to say that one exists without the other, but it is not self-contradictory to suppose:

> The contrary of every matter of fact is still possible; because it can never imply a contradiction and is conceived by the mind with the same facility and distinctness, as if ever so conformable to reality.[5]

---

3. David Hume, *A Treatise of Human Nature*, Book-I, pp. 11-14.
4. Ibid., p. 123.
5. David Hume, *An Enquiry Concerning Human Understanding*, Appendix B; p. 354.

What Hume tries to express is that the opposite of every matter of fact can be conceived with so much confidence as if it were going to be certain. For instance, a matter of fact like "Sun rises in the East" can be refuted by putting forward the statement "tomorrow sun will not rise in the East." These two statements have the same degree of conformity till they are proved in practice. Then Hume questions, why do we think that there is a necessary connection between two events that exist contiguously to each other? Our observation does not provide us with any clue about such a connection. In an attempt to answer this question, Hume asserts that it is because we have so often found that when one of these objects or events is presented to us, the other is presented also. We form the habit of associating them. In fact, this custom or habit, Hume finds, is the source of our idea of necessary connection. Other than this there is no rational proof to show that there exists a necessary connection between two events. Then the only reason we can have for supposing that any two events are connected is that experience (sense-experience) shows them to be so. We may indeed, claims Hume, arrive at such conclusions, prior to our experiencing of them by deducing them from valid theories. But then our only reason for holding these theories to be valid is that they conform to our sense-experience. Hume argues that in any given moment, whatever experience tells us is only, at the best, certain relations between two events consistently obtained in the past. Now the question before us is whether there is any guarantee that nature continues to be uniform. In other words, what guarantee do we have to say that the things which held good in the past will also hold good in future?[6] Thus Hume concludes that we do not have any. Hume, in support of his view, namely, that we do not have any justification to believe in induction, assumes: "We can at least

6. David Hume, *A Treatise of Human Nature*, Book I, p. 135.

conceive a change in the course of nature; which sufficiently proves that such a change is not absolutely impossible."[7] So it is not possible to show that this principle is demonstratively provable. In that case, believes Hume, we can at least show it to be probable, but probability itself must have some ground. All the judgements of probability are to be relied upon past experience. Then, opines Hume, we are caught in a circle, because:

> Probability is founded on the presumption of a resemblance betwixt those objects of which we have had experience, and those of which we have had none; and, therefore, it is impossible this presumption can arise from probability.[8]

It shows that the inference on which we base our beliefs about empirical matters are not formally valid, and the conclusions that we arrive at cannot be shown without circularity even to be probable. We have no justification for believing that things will continue to behave as they have behaved in the past. On Hume's account, we do believe this and act on this supposition as a matter of animal faith, but there is no justification for our doing so.

Ayer's View

But for his style of presentation, we do not think that Ayer's approach is in any way different from that of Hume. Proceeding from the same Humean conception, Ayer puts forward the view that there is no necessary connection between two contiguously existing events. Causation, says Ayer, is a kind of regular sequence that is given in sensory experience. For example, an event "A" causes the event "B" where A and B stand for classes of events. It implies that A is always followed by B. Like his mentor Hume, Ayer too assumes that why we believe in this

7. David Hume, *A Treatise of Human Nature*, p. 136.
8. Ibid., pp. 136-37.

kind of regularity is "this belief is derived from our guiding principle that . . . the future course of our sensations will be in accordance with the past."[9]

Trying to vindicate that this relation of cause and effect is nothing but our imaginative arrangement of facts which are given in sense-experience, Ayer supposes that causal relations are partly factual and partly based on our mental habits. Their factual content is solely dependent on the level at which they operate, i.e. they must correspond with the data given in our sensory experience. The factual content of a singular causal statement is attributed to many aspects such as the assertions of existence, spatio-temporal relations, the states of affairs with which it conjoins and so on. Thus, every singular causal statement may be considered as a universal generalisation; still it can be considered as a statement of tendency.[10]

A universal generalisation, according to Ayer, refers to generalisations like, "All men are mortal" or "All the crows are black." A statement of tendency is that which deals with human affairs, whether on the personal or the social level. For example, whenever my friend yawns, he gets asleep. This shows that the cause of his yawning is his getting asleep. Ayer's main object is to demolish the supposed distinction between universal generalisations and statements of tendency. The distinction between universal generalisations and statements of tendency can be accounted for in terms of our attitude towards them.[11] A few more illustrations of Ayer might help us to understand the notion of causality as propounded by him. On repeated occasions it is found that taking some drug cured a particular disease. There is, argues Ayer, no intrinsic relation between the idea of drug and the idea of cure, but what our sense-experience suggests is that one is always

9. A.J. Ayer, *Language, Truth and Logic*, p. 131.

10. A.J. Ayer, *Probability and Evidence* (London, 1973), pp. 132-33.

11. Ibid., p. 16.

followed by the other. This is what Ayer means by the factual content of a particular causal statement. Accordingly, an association is formed so that the occurrence of one leads to other. In this way, the idea is derived from the habitual conjunction of certain states of affairs in our mind. We tend to transfer our feelings of habituation to them because of an association between cause and effect. Whenever there is an idea of cause, the imagination supplies us a link and we pass on to the effect.

Proceeding further, Ayer asserts that the generalisations of law are not causal. For instance, the functional laws like the law which connects the temperature, volume and pressure of a gas, and taxonomic laws such as the laws that deal with the insects are not causal because we use a kind of causal language that such and such instance is cause of the other. In this connection Ayer classifies causal statements into four important categories. For him, the first category of causal statements consists of the generalisations of law or fact that could be explained by means of a wider theory. The term which is used to "encapsulate" the theory is taken to designate the cause of the phenomena with which a generalisation deals. Certain physical laws like gravitational force, electromagnetic force come under this category of causal statements. The second category of causal statements includes the cases of cause in which the nature of a thing is explained on the basis of its properties. For example, a piece of elastic stretches because it is made of rubber. The third category deals with the cases of causality in which the state of one's own mental condition is the cause of his behaviour. Finally, there are cases of causes where a causal statement links two states of affairs, i.e. two events that can be found at the same observational level. This is the category, according to Ayer, which has philosophical importance.[12]

12. A.J. Ayer, *Probability and Evidence*, p. 133.

The succession of two events in a particular spatio-temporal relation, says Ayer, represents a causal relation between events. Ayer opines that people often misjudge the so-called causal link that is given in sense-experience. Sometimes, it so happens that they identify a trivial state of affairs or a condition to be a cause of a phenomenon. For example, a set of conditions might be responsible for producing another set of conditions (effect). Instead of identifying the entire set as a cause of the phenomenon in question, we isolate one particular condition from the rest and define it by the title cause.[13] The main point of this argument is that when two events or states of affairs follow each other in a particular spatio-temporal relation, it is generally regarded that a particular event or a state of affairs which precedes the effect is termed as the cause and the other as the effect. Why does it so happen? In an attempt to highlight this point, Ayer makes the following observation:

> Sometimes we are rather forced to say that flowers in the garden died because the gardener forgot to water the plants. But, questions Ayer, why should we pick up gardener as the cause of the death of flowers? Anyone would have watered the plant so that they could have survived. Why should we rely only on the gardener for their survival? The immediate answer may be that gardener is expected to do so. This is the reason why we identify him as the cause of the flowers' death. According to Ayer, this is where we go wrong in identifying the cause or causes. There may be many other factors other than gardener's negligence but they are ignored.[14]

Thus the cause and effect, according to Ayer, are nothing but what we choose them to be. It is ridiculous on the part of a professed empiricist like Ayer to dismiss causation as cheaply as this. It is true that we use causal language in our day-to-

13. A.J. Ayer, *Probability and Evidence*, pp. 133-34.

14. Ibid., p. 134.

day dealings but this does not mean that the type of causation that is worked out in scientific investigation to unravel the secrets of Nature, i.e. the laws of Nature, can be reduced to mere causal language. It is evident from the fourfold division of causation that Ayer could not distinguish a causal law from a statement of tendency. This view of Ayer follows from his ontology. Ontologically, what exists for Ayer are sense-data. As has been manifested in the preceding chapter, these sense-data are discrete, unconnected sensory units. They refer to events or matters of fact or state of affairs. In conformity with his ontological claim, Ayer maintains that there is no necessary causal connection between two contiguously existing events. The fourfold divison of causation of Ayer does not represent causation in its perfect sense, i.e. as necessary relation between events in this objective reality.

Trying to further weaken the idea of necessary connection, Ayer writes:

> . . . to those who speak as if there were necessity in the nature is whether they really mean to imply that the laws of Nature are normative rules, enforced by a divine will. If they do not mean to imply this, their talk of necessity is at best an unfortunate metaphor.[15]

It follows from the above statement of Ayer that the belief in necessary causal laws is an unwarranted blind faith. Then causation does not have any objective significance. From Ayer's point of view, what we call causation is our subjective talk of certain phenomena that take place in Nature. If what Ayer says is true then what will happen to science in the absence of necessary causal laws? Scientific laws are not based on tautological truths, but on the necessary relations of cause and effect. Therefore, what is worst affected by Ayer's denial of objective significance of causation is the content of science and

15. A.J. Ayer, *The Foundations of Empirical Knowledge*, p. 198.

its laws. Scientific laws lose their importance and all pretentions to their validity are evaporated. Thus only contingency comes to rule the world of science. Then what, according to Ayer, is science? The only positive answer that he can provide us with is that science is nothing but order and arrangement of our own sense-data which are directly given in sense-experience.

The Problem of Induction

Ayer's conception of causation, namely, that there is no necessary causal connection between events in this reality leads to the problem of induction. The problem of induction is posed in the following way. What justification do we have to give that the things which behaved good in the past are going to behave good in future? The only ground, supposes Ayer, that allows us to tackle this problem is to believe in the principle of uniformity of nature. But, for Ayer, "to speak of the uniformity of nature is to speak of the regularity which it actually displays."[16] However, this regularity is dependent on our imagination. Ayer argues that even if we rely on the principle of uniformity of nature to justify inductive reasoning what guarantee do we have to say that nature will not surprise us anytime. To record Ayer's comments here:

> . . . if there were a law of universal causation a sufficient knowledge of the antecedents of any event would enable us to predict its occurrence. There may still be surprise in store for us because we neither know all the relevant facts, nor have we yet discovered all the laws which govern them.[17]

What is seen in Ayer's approach is a thoroughgoing scepticism. This psychological scepticism of Ayer prevents him from any solution to the so-called problem of induction. Ayer believes that if at all there is a law of universal causation from which

---

16. A.J. Ayer, *The Central Questions of Philosophy*, p. 162.

17. Ibid., p. 161.

we have a sufficient knowledge of causes of any event, then it will enable us to predict its consequents. However genuine our predictions may be, holds Ayer, we are taken by surprise if our predictions go wrong because we are not able to discover the laws that govern them except their law-like character which is observable. The conclusion that Ayer arrives at is that it is not possible to achieve a complete justification on the basis of the principle of uniformity of nature. At the most we can say that all the inductive generalisations are highly probable. In this context Ayer brings in the concept of probability.

What is Probability?

Probability, as a method, is widely used in the field of statistics to study the nature of mass-scale random events. By and large, this method is employed in determining the validity of certain events in the field of mechanics and society. Probability as such is not applicable to well-established scientific laws or laws of Nature. A law does not fail to occur under given conditions. The very edifice of science constitutes such laws of Nature. As pointed out by Keynes, probability expresses a kind of logical relationship between two events. It is not a measure of anything in this reality. The theory of probability studies the properties of mass-scale random events by developing certain mathematical models. There are three important theories of probability. They are: (1) A priori calculus, (2) Frequency theory, and (3) The logical theory and statements of credibility. These three types of probabilities are recognised by positivist philosophers.

The method of a priori calculus can best be illustrated as the gamblers' theory of probability through which gamblers predict certain results. For example, the probability of throwing double six with a true dice is 1/36. It is related to the mathematical calculus of chances. It does not in itself lead us to any conclusion about the likelihood of any event. No scientist would ever rely on such a theory of probability to test his hypotheses. Unlike the theory of a priori calculus, the frequency theory is quite popular in statistics. It is also known as the theory of distribution. For instance, the statement that the probability of an unborn infant will be a girl is more than 50 per cent expresses the relationship of a case belonging to a particular class of cases. This distribution theory of probability is not a mere guess work but a model worked out scientifically to predict certain future events. The logical theory of probability consists of statements of credibility. For instance, there is a probability that the unity in opposition parties in India will throw the ruling party out of power. Such statements of credibility are purely based on logical interpretation of a particular situation where reason dominates the scene. In some cases the statements of credibility are dependent on statistical statements, but they are not statistical statements by themselves. Whatever may be the results of applicability of the above-said theories of probability, the concept of probability does not have any role to play in establishing the existence of certain laws of Nature.

It is so unfortunate that Ayer applies the concept of probability to all the statements of law without recognising their objective significance in the course of scientific investigation. He holds that an observation increases our confidence in the statement in question irrespective of its status. Even the statements of law are not exceptions so far as the probability is concerned.[18] It implies that the degree in the increase or decrease of probability of a particular proposition (here the proposition refers to a matter of fact), depends on its occurrence which is given in sensory experience. The probability of any proposition is derived from the past experience. Thus, Ayer justifies Humean conception that we cannot prove inductive reasoning unless it is given in sense-experience.

---

18. A.J. Ayer, *Language, Truth and Logic*, p. 132.

To sum up, the whole theory of causation of Ayer from which the problem of induction has emerged rests on the arrangements of certain events that are given in sense-experience. It denies the necessary causal connection between events since such connection is not given in sense-experience. In short, the active power on the part of cause is denied. On this view of causation, to talk of cause is entirely different from giving a reason why it does not explain that certain effects have resulted from certain causes. It only informs us what preceded the effect. From this analysis of causation, it is evident that Ayer's view stands in glaring contradiction to actual scientific view of causation. The problem of induction and subjective interpretation of causation has been criticised on different grounds. For the sake of brevity, we are not going to present all those criticisms that are directed against the problem of induction and subjectivity of causation, but only those which are considered to be very important from our standpoint.

As early as in 1945 the German logician Carl Gustuv Hempel[19] in his very famous article entitled "Studies in the Logic of Confirmation I & II" tries to show that inductive reasoning often violates intuition. He cites an interesting raven paradox to highlight the problem of induction. He tries to illustrate the paradox by putting forward the following hypothesis:

1. All ravens are black.

According to the law of implication, in strict logical terms, this statement is equivalent to:

2. Everything that is not black is not a raven.

Therefore, in all circumstances where (2) is true, (1) is also true. Similarly, in all circumstances where (2) is false, (1) is also false. Such a similarity establishes logical equivalence. Given a

19. Carl Hempel, "Studies in the Logic of Confirmation I & II", *Mind* (London, 1945), vol. 54, nos. 213-14 pp. 1, 97.

general statement such as "All ravens are black," we can consider a form of the same statement that refers to a specific observable instance of the general class to constitute evidence for that general statement. For example:

3. Nevermore, my pet raven is black.

This example supports the hypothesis that "All ravens are black." But the paradox occurs when the same process is applied to statement (2). By seeing a green apple, we can observe:

4. This green (and thus not black) thing is an apple (and thus not a raven).

By the same reasoning, this statement has the evidence that (2) Everything that is not black is not a raven. But this statement is logically equivalent to (1) All ravens are black, it follows that the sight of a green apple offers evidence that all ravens are black. This is precisely the problem of induction, according to Hempel.

There is another interesting twist to the problem of induction raised by Nelson Goodman[20] in his famous "New Riddle of Induction" in his *Fact, Fiction, and Forecast* in 1954 concerning the concept of confirmation or prediction. He calls it the paradox of prediction. According to Goodman, it is always possible to define a vocabulary in such a way that when given a choice between two possibilities, it is likely that the possibility which runs counter to previous or past experience will be chosen as the more predictable one. To illustrate this apparent breakdown in reasoning, Goodman devised a new predicate called "grue" to show that given a choice between two separate provable statements that all emeralds were green and all emeralds were Blue, he argues instead that all emeralds were in fact "grue." The colour "grue" is applied to all things

20. Nelson Goodman, *Fact, Fiction and Forecast* (Indianapolis, 1965), 2nd edn., pp. 32-34.

that are observed before time *t* and found to be green, and to those things which are blue and observed after time *t*. If the emeralds which are observed before time *t* are green. But they also confirm the hypothesis that all emeralds are grue. This results in a riddle that the emeralds observed after time *t* should be grue and hence blue. Certainly, the critics have quickly pointed out that unlike green, grue is not a natural colour. Both green and grue may have similar linguistic form, but internally they are two different concepts. Green as a colour implies a similarity between its past and present instances, but "grue" suggests a change of colour over a period of time. Therefore, green and grue cannot be equated with each other, for the latter is not a genuinely qualitative predicate.

Critical Reflections

Immanuel Kant, while criticising Hume's theory of causation, holds the view that the idea of necessary connection is not given in sense-experience. To that extent Hume is right. But, unlike Hume, Kant does not reduce causation to a mere subjective enterprise. Kant says that the idea of necessary connection is known a priori. To put it in Kantian terminology:

> If an example from the sciences be desired, we have only to look to any of the propositions of mathematics, if we seek an example from the understanding in its quite ordinary employment, the proposition, "every alteration must have a cause," will serve our purpose. In the latter case indeed, the very concept of a cause so manifestly contains the concept of a necessity of connection. . . .[21]

Kant's use of the term "cause" has a special meaning. The very term "cause" as a concept, holds Kant, retains the idea of necessary connection within it. One need not derive this idea

---

21. Immanuel Kant, *Critique of Pure Reason*, tr. N.K.P. Smith, abridged edn., p. 27.

of necessary connection from any empirical source. Every attempt to derive the idea of necessary connection from mere empirical experiences results in pure subjective necessity. For he considers that the causal necessity, though known a priori, is certainly objective. Thus, Kant justifies the objective significance of causal connections and their significance in explaining Hume's subjective necessity of causal connection, is equally applicable to Ayer's theory, since Ayer is an ideal follower of David Hume.

A.N. Whitehead, the twentieth-century mathematician and metaphysician, in defence of necessary causal connection, holds the view that Hume's philosophy is inadequate to explain the necessary causal connection that exists between two events. Finding fault with Humean analysis of causation, Whitehead, in line with his philosophy of organism, maintains that Hume, instead of deriving "presentational immediacy" from "causal efficacy" tries to explain "causal efficacy" in terms of "presentational immediacy." According to Whitehead, Hume's refusal of necessary causal connection is dependent on the dogma that all the percepts are reduced to presentational immediacy. Whitehead questions the very foundations of Humean causation by arguing, if what we call causation is derived from custom or habit then:

> . . . how can a "habit" be felt, when a "cause" cannot be felt? Is there any presentational immediacy in the feeling of a "habit?" Hume by sleight of hand confuses a habit of feeling blinks after flashes with a "feeling of the habit of feeling blinks after flashes."[22]

Whitehead is very logical in his approach. If the cause is not given in sense-experience, then why a habit be given in sense-

22. A.N. Whitehead, "Experiencing Causal Connection", in *Philosophic Problems*, ed. Maurice Mandelbaum, p. 120.

experience? One cannot have different yardsticks to explain the notion of "cause" and the notion of "habit." Though Whitehead's objection to Hume's theory does not have much epistemological importance, it has greater logical importance. Ayer's theory is no exception to Whitehead's criticism.

Karl Popper[23], on the other hand, claims to have solved the problem of induction that has cropped up from Hume's theory of causation. He classifies Hume's problem into logical and psychological. According to the logical version of the problem, "Are we justified in reasoning from (repeated) instances of which we have experience to other instances (conclusions) of which we have no experience?" No. This is the answer of Hume. The psychological version of the problem is, "Are we justified in" reasoning from (repeated) instances of which we have experience to the probability of other instances (conclusions) of which we have no experience? What Popper wants to show is that these two problems clash with each other.

Popper laments that Hume who is supposed to be one of the greatest rational minds, turned out to be a sceptic and irrational epistemologist by converting the logical problem of induction into a psychological one. Popper claims to have approached the problem of induction by translating all the subjective and psychological terms into objective terms. He prefers to replace the expression "belief" with "statement" or "explanatory theory," "impression" with "observation statement," and "justification of a belief" with "justification of the claim that a theory is true." This kind of the principle of transference, argues Popper, would solve the logical problem of induction. Once the logical problem of induction is resolved, the psychological problem, which is akin to logical one, can also be solved. So far as the logical problem of induction is concerned, holds Popper, it is true that any number of positive

23. Karl Popper, *Objective Knowledge* (London, 1979), pp. 3-6.

observational statements can never guarantee the truth of the explanatory universal theory. But, supposes Popper, that there is another variety of logical problem. He poses the question in the following manner:

> Can the claim that an explanatory universal theory is true or that it is false be justified by "empirical reasons?" that is, can the assumption of the truth of test statements justify either the claim that a universal theory is true or the claim that it is false?[24]

Popper's answer to this problem is positive. He claims that it is possible to justify the claim that an explanatory universal theory may be shown to be false. Thus, Popper claims to have solved the problem of induction.

However significant Popper's solution may be, it is evident that Popper is mainly concerned with the clarification of linguistic confusions that arise in the problem of induction. His theory of transference would only restate the problem of induction in an objectivist language. Just by doing so, it does not mean the problem of induction is solved. The problem of induction is not a logical problem, as conceived by Popper, but a practical one. Apart from that, every logical problem ultimately boils down to a psychological one.

P.F. Strawson is another British logician who vehemently opposed the view that the problem of induction can be justified by reducing it to a kind of deductive reasoning. He conceives that any reasoning that is derived from an inductive premise or from the axioms of the calculus of probability would ultimately lead us to the view that induction is based on induction. More than that, any attempt to justify that by its success in experience will lead us to the assumption that what held good in the past will also hold good in future.[25]

24. Karl Popper, *Objective Knowledge*, p. 7.

25. P.F. Strawson, *Introduction to Logical Theory* (Delhi, 1976), pp. 248-50.

The modest way, according to Strawson, is to ask whether it is reasonable to rely on inductive arguments. In such cases, feels Strawson, the answer is always positive, since "being reasonable" means having a degree of confidence or belief in a particular statement depending upon the strength of the evidence available in favour of that particular statement. It shows that the reasonableness of induction, claims Strawson, is analytic, because it is proportionate to its evidence. Then the question whether inductive reasoning in general is justified is like asking whether law of the land is legal.[26]

Another notable objection against the problem of induction comes from Gilbert Ryle.[27] In his article entitled "Induction and Hypothesis" Ryle attacks the view that universal generalisations are highly probable. He argues that scientists' propositions cannot be hypotheses or probabilities, since they are well established truths or falsehoods. He holds the view that the propositions of science are not commands, signals, statements or recommendation of habits. Hence, it is a mistake to describe a scientific proposition as mere hypothesis or probable. Ryle maintains that the propositions of science are established to be explanations of others which are known to be true. These, according to Ryle, are called "laws" and not hypotheses.

The other objection that Ryle raises is that generally inductive arguments are directed to cover the unobserved and future events. But in this process, claims Ryle, some philosophers link up the problem of induction with the "prediction" of future, i.e. we look for rational justification of this problem on the basis of predictions. Ryle argues, for instance, take the proposition "All swans are white," from this we can predict

26. P.F. Strawson, *Introduction to Logical Theory*, p. 257.

27. Gilbert Ryle, "Induction and Hypothesis", in his *Collected Papers*, p. 131.

that all the swans which are unobserved turn out to be white. But Ryle holds that our predictions have extra precariousness which may lead us to:

> Contradict someone's prediction of an eclipse not only by denying the truth of his law-propositions or the truth of his observations of the contemporary heavens, but also denying that there will exist a sun, moon, and earth at the required date.[28]

Thus Ryle concludes that if we rely upon the predictions, the founts of instances to which our scientific laws relied on to apply, may be ignored completely. The other objection of Ryle is directed against the view that: What justification do we have to give that some inductions are stronger than others? This question is wrongly posed. His answer is that we cannot call an argument as inductive unless it has some reliability in the generalisation in question. He writes:

> An induction of zero reliability is, I think, as much impossibility as a fallacious deduction. A fallacious deduction is not a deduction; and induction based on no empirical evidence or containing a contradiction is no induction.[29]

Ryle declares that the question of justification of induction does not arise, since all inductive arguments are relied on empirical evidence.

The criticisms levelled against the problem of induction clearly show that the so-called problem of induction is our own creation. As such there is no problem of induction.

From the standpoint of scientific realism, science is based on the postulates of necessary connection between cause and effect. It implies that causation is the real essence of things. Since Ayer's

---

28. P.F. Strawson, op. cit., p. 134.

29. Ibid., p. 147.

epistemology limits the scope of human cognitive activity by reducing it to mere appearances (sense-data) it cannot explain the objective reality in terms of necessary causal connections which play an important role in the scientific investigation.

As a rule, scientific investigation is directed towards the disclosure of the specific causes of the phenomena. For instance, in the field of medicine investigations are going on to find the cause of cancer. This clearly tells us how science is deeply interested in finding out the necessity of certain causal connections that exist among the phenomena. It is through the cause and effect relation that a scientist tries to make certain assumptions about the nature of reality. But philosophers like Ayer declare that necessity is a conventional postulate accepted by the people as a reference point to facilitate explanation of reality. There is nothing in nature, maintains Ayer, that corresponds to this postulate. Nature does not have to behave to suit our interests. These philosophers have reduced causation to the level of a mere repetition of certain events whereby an antecedent event is called cause and the consequent as effect. For example, day follows night and night follows day. How do we know which is the cause of the other? One can interpret this particular situation according to his own taste. But the real cause of this day and night is the rotation of earth around the sun. This point disqualifies the view that mere succession in time is an adequate sign of cause. The most important thing to notice is that a cause by itself may be the effect of some other phenomena, and the same effect may be the cause of some other phenomena. Thus what is characteristic of causation is the endless chain of reciprocal connections, the universal interaction of objects and phenomena of the reality, where each link turns out to be both a cause and an effect. In this connection it is necessary to mention the role of chance events which play a vital role in causation. All the above-mentioned aspects of causation are denied by Ayer and other logical positivists.

The concept of chance and probability can be discussed only in the context of causation. Causation is the most general and universal relation that exists among the phenomena. Chance events play an important role in causation. What is called chance in the context of one set of phenomena may be the cause in another set of phenomena. For example, we know that under given conditions a seed will germinate. Its failure to germinate results from the failure of one of the ingredients that provide conditions for its germination. Then there must be a cause for the absence of that particular condition. Thus, a chance event has its own cause. As a matter of fact, it is evident from the above example that necessity follows the essence and the internal nature of the developing phenomena. It is constant and stable. On the contrary, a chance event in opposition to necessity may not happen frequently. Chance event is purely an external condition and it is unstable and temporary. The whole discussion reveals that a "law" does not fail to occur under given conditions.

Necessity realises itself through a series of chance events. At the same time chance events are governed by an internal necessity. Further it requires that our knowledge should not only be the knowledge of the inevitable but also of probable. For instance, from a given process we must not only know what effect necessarily follows from what cause but we must also know the probabilities of various causes coming into operation and various effects following. This helps us to judge how to act in order to control the whole process including chance events. In this respect probable knowledge expresses our expectation of the occurrence of chance events. But for Ayer probability is mere subjective enquiry in the sense that a judgement of probability is an expression of nothing but our subjective uncertainty or lack of knowledge of necessary connection between events.

From the above analysis of causation, we can conclude that

Ayer misinterpreted the nature of causation and its belated offspring, namely, the problem of induction by denying the necessary causal connections between the events of the objective reality.

7

On Other Minds and Statements about the Past

Knowledge of other minds is another important epistemological problem that constantly plagues logical positivists. Like any other problem in the history of philosophy, the problem of knowledge of other minds has considerably attracted the attention of many philosophers. This problem is intimately connected with the principle of verification. As pointed out elsewhere the fundamental tenet of this principle is that whatever knowledge we acquire must, in the final analysis, terminate in sense-experience. In other words, the principle sets limits to the scope of human knowledge by confining itself to the apparent features of the phenomena. This assumption leads to the problem of knowledge of other minds, namely, what justification do we have to believe that there are minds other than ours? Do others have feelings of pleasure or pain like us? If they do have, are they accessible to us? If yes, how to know them? Of all the above questions, the last one appears to be very interesting to the philosophers. If one employs verification (having sensory experiences of some sort) as a method to have the knowledge of other minds then the problem becomes more accute, since the principle is construed in such a way that it cannot go beyond the appearances. This ill-equipped principle of logical positivists ultimately leads to scepticism and solipsism. Knowing the consequences of this principle, Ayer tries to approach the problem of knowledge of other minds through phenomenalistic analysis of self, telepathy and argument from analogy. Much to his discomfort, all the methods proved futile. Similarly, the problem of knowledge of statements about the past is an epistemological problem that haunted logical positivists. Ayer poses the question: Is it possible for us to have direct acquaintance with the past? Ayer tries to approach this problem through memory and temporal succession in time. In spite of his valient attempts, Ayer could not solve this problem, since it is more of a psychological nature than methodological.

In this chapter, the prime concern is to show that Ayer with his ontological and epistemological framework cannot escape from scepticism and solipsism. Being an avowed empiricist with Humean legacy, Ayer prepares the ground in such a way that it cannot overcome scepticism. He feels that any problem is claimed to have been solved provided it satisfies a sceptic (not a Cartesian sceptic), since sceptic's horns are very strong. Let us discuss these issues in detail.

The problem of knowledge of other minds cannot be understood without understanding the notion of self as expounded by Ayer. As a matter of fact, Ayer endorsed Humean conception of self. Hume's notion of self follows his ontology. It is appropriate here to give a brief sketch of Humean notion of self. With regard to the notion of self, Ayer admits, "our reasoning on this point, as on so many others, is in conformity with Hume's."[1]

The Notion of "Self"

As shown in the first chapter while discussing the development of empiricism, for Hume the idea of substance in any form is meaningless. Likewise, says Hume, the idea of self is also meaningless. Hume writes in his *Treatise* as follows:

1. A.J. Ayer, *Language, Truth, and Logic*, p. 167.

> When we talk of self or substance we must have an idea annexed to these terms, otherwise they are altogether unintelligible. Every idea is derived from preceding impressions; and we have no impression of self or substance, as something simple and individual. We have, therefore, no idea of them in that sense.[2]

Hume maintains that there is no impression from which the idea of self can be derived, since there is no impression that is continuous and invariable. What then, according to Hume, does this self consist of? He argues that there is no such simple and continued principle in me. In defence of his argument, Hume illustrates this point by saying:

> . . . When I enter most intimately into what I call myself, I always stumble on some particular perception or other, of heat . . . or pleasure. I can never catch myself at any time without a perception, and never observe anything but the perception.[3]

For Hume self consists of a bundle of sense-impressions (perceptions) which succeed one another with an unimaginable rapidity and flow. Hume denies the view that there is a substantive "self" on the ground that no such entity is ever observable. The same phenomenalistic approach towards "self" has been advocated by Ayer. Like Hume, Ayer too reduces self to sense-contents or sense-data. He holds the view: "We know that a self, if it is not to be treated as a metaphysical entity, must be held to be a logical construction out of sense-experience."[4]

As it has been shown earlier, Ayer reduces all the material or physical objects to sense-contents or sense-data. For, he

---

2. David Hume, *A Treatise of Human Nature*, p. 358.
3. Ibid., pp. 301-2.
4. A.J. Ayer, *Language, Truth and Logic*, p. 165

opines that material objects are nothing but logical constructs out of actual and possible sense-data. A similar view is expressed by Ayer with regard to the nature of self. Further he holds that these sense-experiences out of which the notion of "self" is derived must belong to the sense-history of the same self. According to Ayer, no two selves can share the same experience. In other words, no two persons can share the same sense-contents, since each one's experiences are private to oneself. This very notion of Ayer leads to privacy of experiences, and consequently to solipsism.

Ayer opens up the issue by arguing that it is commonly held by philosophers that each person's mental states or events are private to himself. The thoughts, feelings, dreams, imagination, pain and pleasure, sensations and memories are only accessible to the person who is experiencing them. He maintains that we cannot have any inroads into others' feelings. The only way, contests Ayer, to know them is through communication. One can communicate one's feelings to his fellow beings but he cannot transfer his feelings to them.[5] Proceeding further, Ayer maintains that generally people claim that they have perceived the same object, but it is not so. Their perceptions may be qualitatively alike, but numerically different in the sense that the object perceived by them is certainly a public one. However, the experiences undergone by each person while perceiving the object are private to one's own self. To quote Ayer in this context:

> It is maintained . . . that two different persons perceiving the same physical object is "really" a matter of each one's sensing his own sense-data; and these sense-data, though they may be similar, cannot be the same. And so we reach the philosophical contention that all one's experiences are private to oneself.[6]

5. A.J. Ayer, *The Problem of Knowledge*, p. 199.
6. Ibid., pp. 199-200.

From the above passage of Ayer it follows that the extent to which a person knows about himself is private. For example, if my states of mind are essentially private to me, how can others have any knowledge of them? Thus the logical extreme of this assertion is solipsism, the doctrine that everything I know is private to me so that I am in some way locked up in my own subjective world. This privacy of experiences leads Ayer to the problem of knowledge of other minds. Attempting to solve this problem, Ayer enumerates various solutions. Let us examine these various attempts of Ayer to solve the problem of other minds.

Phenomenalistic Analysis

Ayer advocates this reductive analysis of self in his *Language, Truth and Logic*. He tries to reduce the existence of other people to one's own sense-contents. According to this analysis, the nature of other people can be interpreted ". . . in terms of their empirical manifestations, that is, in terms of the behaviour of their bodies, and ultimately in terms of sense-contents."[7]

Now the question that arises is: Whose sense-contents? Certainly these sense-contents cannot be anyone else's, for it would be absurd to say that I know that such and such a person exists because his bodily behaviour is manifested in the sense-contents belonging to my sense-history. These sense-contents, according to Ayer, which are relevant to one's knowledge of the existence of other people must, then, be his own. Trying to clarify this point, Ayer argues that I know that there are other people because: ". . . my hypothesis is verified by the occurrence in my sense-history of the appropriate series of sense-contents."[8]

---

7. A.J. Ayer, *Language, Truth and Logic*, p. 171.

8. Ibid.

This view of Ayer cannot escape from solipsism, because the assumption that Mr "X" exists is equivalent to saying that I know that I have certain sense-data in which Mr X's behaviour is presented. On this account of Ayer, we are led to the impression that one can never know anything except his own sense-contents. Thus Ayer concludes: ". . . each of us has to define the contents of another man's sense-experience in terms of what he can himself observe."[9]

Ayer firmly believes that it is one of the ways of justifying the existence of other people by reducing them to their bodily behaviour. However, there is another difficulty that comes in Ayer's way that is scepticism. Being an ardent supporter of Humean empiricism Ayer gives scepticism its proper place in his doctrines. He rejects this phenomenalistic approach to other minds on the ground that one can distinguish his own thoughts, feelings and their outward manifestations, but there is no way for him to distinguish others' thoughts, feelings and their outward manifestations because all that one can observe is the physical manifestation of other people's behaviour. To quote Ayer's remarks in this context:

> There can be empirical grounds for inferring the occurrence of behaviour, on the part of other people, which one is not actually observing, inasmuch as it is logically conceivable that one should observe it, but there cannot, on this view, be any empirical grounds for inferring the existence of anything "behind" this behaviour of which it might be supposed to be an external manifestation.[10]

Ayer concedes the point that from the physical manifestations of the other people's behaviour we cannot infer the existence of anything that is not given in one's own sense-contents. Ayer faces this problem constantly because of his weak

9. A.J. Ayer, *Language, Truth and Logic*, p. 174.

10. A.J. Ayer, *The Foundations of Empirical Knowledge*, p. 163.

epistemological framework. His principle of verification, which is supposed to be the backbone of his epistemology, is restricted to appearances alone. In fact, Ayer faces the same problem in other instances also.

Telepathy

Telepathy is a form of extra-sensory perception through which one can introspect into others' minds. Ayer presupposes that if one can approach the problem of knowledge of other minds telepathically we will be able to reach some solution. The characteristic feature of telepathy, holds Ayer, is that one can introspect into thoughts of others directly, without employing any physical means. Nevertheless, argues Ayer:

> . . . to be informed of another's feelings telepathically is not to share it; and even if it were to share it, there would be exactly the same grounds here as in the case of any other's shared feelings for saying that there were two feelings and not one.[11]

What follows the above argument of Ayer is that even the telepathic experiences are private to one's own self. The person who practises telepathy can know what is going on in other's mind, but he cannot share his feelings or thoughts. In this case again the knowledge of other minds will exhaust in between two people — the person who is experiencing them and the person who practises telepathy. This approach towards the problem of knowledge of other minds, laments Ayer, is no better than a telephonic conversation between two persons.[12]

What is spurious about Ayer's argument is that he tries to show that one cannot share the views or feelings or thoughts of others. That does not mean that there is no way to find out

---

11. A.J. Ayer, "One's Knowledge of Other Minds", in his *Philosophical Essays* (London, 1965), p. 196.
12. Ibid.

what is happening in the minds of others. The question of sharing others' mental phenomena does not arise since each individual retains his privacy of experiences. An ardent sceptic might argue that since there is no possibility of sharing others' feelings or thoughts, there is no possibility of establishing their existence. This is against common-sense viewpoint. No one would ever say that since I have not seen Delhi, I do not believe in the existence of such a city in India. In this regard a philosopher is not an exception.

Then the last method left for Ayer to solve this alleged problem of other minds is through the argument from analogy.

The Argument from Analogy

The argument from analogy, as it is generally considered, holds between two dissimilar objects. According to this argument, the establishment of similarity or resemblance in certain respects like properties and relations between two different kinds of objects gives rise to the belief that both the objects are more or less similar with regard to their anatomy. Ayer applies this argument to the problem of knowledge of other minds.

The argument from analogy, as expounded by Ayer, proceeds from the assumption that it is supposed that as we note the connections between our own states of mind and their outward expressions, likewise we also notice these outward expressions in others. Hence, there must be some connection between their outward expressions and states of mind. Trying to illustrate the possibility of analogy, Ayer argues:

> By analogy with what I have observed of other people and what I have learnt about myself, I infer that someone with the relevant sort of nervous system, when operated on in such and such conditions, will show signs of pain, signs that I may well be able to detect if I watch him closely enough. But then I want to go further and argue from the existence of

> these signs to the existence of his actual feeling of pain, which *ex hypothesi*, since it is not my feeling, I cannot detect.[13]

To exemplify it with an instance of pain, the argument follows in this way. When I am having an infected tooth, I go to a dentist and get it removed. In such a condition, I maintain that my feeling of pain, when dentist operates on me, will provide me with a reason for believing that my friend, i.e. a person other than myself, feels pain when the dentist operates on him. However, the pain experienced by me and pain experienced by my friend cannot be the same. The only reason, claims Ayer, for me to believe that he is in pain is that I too experienced similar kind of pain when I was operated on.

Ayer says that the quick way with this argument is that an argument from analogy cannot be used when there is no possibility, even in principle, to determine independently whether other minds exist. There is no justification for the supposition that a body in front of me belongs to someone other than myself. An argument from analogy, on this account, is valid only when there is a possibility of establishing the existence of other minds independently. But in the present case there is no such possibility. The futility of argument from analogy is expressed by Ayer in the following manner:

> An important consequence of this argument, if it is sound, is that we must give up the argument from analogy on which many people have relied as a justification for believing in the existence of other minds. It is tempting to think that one can come of the idea of one's own experiences of certain kinds are characteristically associated with certain forms of behaviour. . . . Assuming it is logically impossible for anyone directly to observe what goes on in another person's mind, some philosophers have maintained that this is not a valid argument from analogy, for they hold that no inductive

13. A.J. Ayer, op. cit., p. 202.

> argument can give us any reason to believe in the existence of something which could not even in principle be observed.[14]

The reason why the argument from analogy cannot justify the belief in the existence of other minds is very simple. Ayer's principle of verification is designed in such a way that it will not entertain any form of knowledge other than what is given in sense-experience. If one applies this principle to the problem of knowledge of other minds, it is evident that one cannot have any sense-experience, even in principle, which can support the belief that there are minds other than one's own. The only way to know what is happening in the minds of others is to reduce their mental happenings to the perceptible behaviour of them. But there is no way to go beyond this perceptible behaviour of outward manifestations. Then it is nothing but flogging a dead horse. Knowing quite well that it is impossible to satisfy a sceptic, Ayer went on trying method after method to solve this problem. In this process all that he could prove is that none can satisfy a sceptic.

Critical Reflections

Several philosophers have thrown light on this problem of knowledge of other minds. Perhaps they are apparently successful in their attempts, since they have not given any importance to scepticism. They approached this problem more methodically in order to clear away the misconceptions that come in the way. The notable among them are Carnap, Ryle and Austin.

As early as in 1934 Carnap advocated physicalism. According to this thesis, every possible experience can be converted into a physicalistic language which is public. Since

14. A.J. Ayer, "The Concept of a Person", in his *The Concept of a Person and Other Essays* (London, 1973), p. 87.

the language is intersubjective, it is easy to communicate the structural aspects of phenomena. To put it more clearly, the behavioural aspects of a person, which are directly accessible to anyone's observation, represent his mental states such as thoughts, feelings or sensations or private experiences of any kind. Carnap obviously makes a distinction between "physicalistic language" and "protocol language." The statements of protocol language refer to one's own private experiences, while the statements of physicalistic language refer to public objects or processes. Carnap introduces a kind of reductionism which is not akin to phenomenalism. The reductionism of Carnap tries to reduce all protocol statements to physicalistic statements which are directly observable. The main idea behind this physicalistic analysis of other minds is that intersubjective physical language can refer to the contents of one's own private experiences. However, Carnap admits that "there is no solution free from contradictions."[15]

Perhaps what is anticipated by Carnap is that true reduction is not possible in all cases. But he did not advocate scepticism. To Carnap's mind, at least, there is a chance of projecting one's mind to the public world.

Ryle, on the other hand, argues against the view that it is impossible to provide a satisfactory evidence that there exist minds other than one's own. For he considers that one's ways of knowing his own mental acts are the same as his ways of knowing the mental acts of others. Ryle says: "The sorts of things that I can find out about myself are the same as the sorts of things that I can find out about other people."[16] In order to illustrate this point, Ryle maintains that generally people believe that they are "conscious" of their own doings, but it is a wrong notion. For instance, argues Ryle, when I

15. Rudolf Carnap, *The Unity of Science* (London, 1934), p. 82.

16. G. Ryle, *The Concept of Mind*, p. 149.

"wonder" what is the possible answer to a puzzle it is like saying that I am performing two sorts of things at a time — one is solving the puzzle and the other is wondering about it. In other words, it is to say that my act of wondering and its self-intimation are two different things which are joined together. Ryle exemplifies it by saying:

> . . . Mental processes are phosphorescent, like tropical sea water, which makes itself visible with the light which it itself emits. Or, to use another simile, mental processes are overheard by the mind whose processes they are, somewhat as a speaker overhears the words he is himself uttering.[17]

Against this theory of "phosphorescence," namely, one is conscious of his own doings, Ryle advocates the view that generally we know what we are about. There is no need of any self-intimation of our own doings to our minds. Similarly, we know what other people are about. There is no need for us to introspect into their minds' happenings. The theories of consciousness and introspection, asserts Ryle, are myths.

The other issue to be settled is how to know that there are other minds. Ryle contests that we can discover that there are minds other than our own by understanding what others communicate to us. He maintains that there are many occasions when we appreciate the doings of other people in many ways. This does not mean, holds Ryle, that we are inferring the workings of other's mind. For instance, when a person cracks a joke others appreciate it. Likewise, when two persons play a chess game one understands the chess stratagems of the other. This shows that we follow the minds of others by their actions. Ryle concludes the whole issue by saying:

> To find that most people have minds (though idiots and infants in the arms do not) is simply to find that they are

17. G. Ryle, *The Concept of Mind*, p. 152.

> prone to do certain sorts of things, and this we do by witnessing the sorts of things they do. Indeed we do not merely discover that there are other minds, we discover what specific qualities of intellect and character particular people have.[18]

Ryle's approach towards the knowledge of the working of other minds sounds very logical. Scepticism in its limited dose may not hamper the proceedings of any philosophic inquiry. If it transcends its limits then it leads us nowhere.

Austin's celebrated essay "Other Minds" which is supposed to have received an unqualified acclaim, deals with the problem of knowledge of other minds from the standpoint of ordinary language philosophy. Austin's main contention is to show what sort of things do actually happen when a common man asks: How do you know? Is this really so and so? Why do you believe it? He feels that it is a matter of everyday experience that we claim to know other people. Austin's treatment of the problem is based more on the view as to how people interpret the word "know" in their day-to-day dealings. He feels that philosophers have not paid much attention to the minute of how words are actually used.

Austin tries to compare the locution "I promise" with the locution "I know." He opines that knowing that Tom looks angry does not mean that I know him. In this sense of knowing a person, argues Austin, means how he looks like or knowing what may be described. Austin's basic concern is to show that uttering such words is an act of performance of a certain ritual which shows one's relation to others. As Austin puts it, when I say "I promise," I am not simply giving my assurance to anybody what I intend to do, but by using this formula, performing this ritual, I have committed myself to others, and

18. G. Ryle, op. cit., p. 59.

staked my reputation in a new way.[19] Proceeding further, Austin maintains:

> Similarly, saying "I know" is taking a new plunge. But it is now saying "I have performed a special striking feat of cognition, superior, in the same scale as believing and being sure, even to being merely quite sure," for there is nothing in that scale superior to being quite sure. Just promising is not something superior, in the same scale as hoping and intending, even to merely fully intending: for there is nothing that scale superior to fully intending. When I say "I know," I give others my word: I give others my authority for saying that "S is P."[20]

Austin's contention is to bring out the intricacies involved in the utterance I know that "S is P." He argues that to know something is not to be understood as a description of that something in question. It is more than that. To know something is a performatory utterance. In other words, when someone says that I know that "S is P" what he meant by that is that he knew it. To suppose that "I know" is only a descriptive phrase is to commit a descriptive fallacy,[21] according to which words are used to describe things or events. Thus Austin compares the locution "I know" with "I promise."[22]

R.M. Chisholm quickly picks a hole in Austin's argument. According to him, what is wrong with Austin's approach is that Austin underestimated the descriptive use of the words. The locution "I know," holds Chisholm, not only performs a

---

19. J.L. Austin, "Other Minds", in his *Philosophical Papers*, ed. J.O. Urmson and G.J. Warnock (London, 1970), p. 99.

20. Ibid.

21. Ibid., p. 103.

22. According to Pritchard, "I promise" is neither true nor false. It is a kind of linguistic mechanism by which the speaker imposes an obligation on himself.

ritual, but also describes the ritual in question. He opines that the descriptive and the performative uses of the word are compatible with each other. To suppose that a performative use of words prevents its descriptive use, asserts Chisholm, it might well be called a performative fallacy.[23]

As opposed to Ayer's views, the philosophers like Carnap, Ryle, Austin and Chisholm have rightly shown that we do have knowledge of other minds. Now the question before us is not the treatment of the problem, but to find out the cause of the problem. Then we have to analyse this problem realistically. As we have discussed, the problem of knowledge of other minds is intimately connected with Ayer's treatment of the notion of "self." Like Hume, Ayer denies the existence of a substantial self. He gives a phenomenalistic account of the self, according to which self is nothing but a bundle of sense-data or sense-contents. Certainly, it is not the case. To explain the notion of self which is identified with the letter "I" one has to proceed in the following way.

When we want to establish the intuitive clarity of the awareness of our consciousness, i.e. to be aware of oneself, one must be able to see, hear, smell, feel, experience, and understand. But the ability of doing these things, in the final analysis, is the characteristic feature of a sentient being. Thus we arrive at the idea of "I see," "I hear," "I feel" and so on. A person is one who calls himself "I." He feels pain, pleasure, anger, love, hatred and so on. He calls himself "I" because he is aware of his own presence in this phenomenal world along with other persons and things surrounding him. It is rather foolish to ask him, how does he know that he is existing? How does he know that others are existing? One must realise that a person who calls "himself" is a body that acts and thinks and

---

23. R.M. Chisholm, *Theory of Knowledge* (New Delhi, 1977), 2nd edn., pp. 127-32.

is perceived by other persons as well. He is not a mysterious entity. Similarly, other people are not mysterious to him. In this way, we can define a self as an active thinking body capable of knowing several things about itself, and others. The communication between one person and the other is possible through the means of language provided that there is some other person who sees, hears and understands it. Thus language is not only public, but also intersubjective. This public language is used to refer to the private experiences of a person. There is nothing like a private language. Experiences are private to one's own self. That does not mean that they are not meaningfully communicated to others at all. From the standpoint of science, the problem of knowledge of other minds is a pseudo-problem. Had there been such a problem in the past, there would have been anarchy of human affairs.

Statements about the Past

The problem of statements about the past is connected with the principle of verification of A.J. Ayer. As it is shown, the principle of verification in the final analysis rests on the view that meaning of a statement is the fact that is given in one's sensory experience. A person verifies a statement when he has such sensory experience. Accordingly, I understand the meaning of a statement only when I have experienced certain sense-data related to that statement in question. On a plausible interpretation of the principle it must be metaphysical to say that something happened at a time when "I" was still unborn. I being still unborn could not have witnessed it and that on the same interpretation of the principle it appears metaphysical for me to say that there are sense-experiences which are not mine. This conception of Ayer leads to the problem of statements about the past.

Ayer questions, how can we justify the claim that there are statements about the past, other than shifting historical records? According to Ayer, there is no possibility of direct acquaintance with the past events. Perhaps, holds Ayer, memory could be taken into consideration as a bridge between the past and present. He maintains: ". . . that memory is a form of knowledge is constructed as implying the possibility of direct acquaintance with the past, that it continues."[24]

However, the quick way of this argument, claims Ayer, is that remembering a particular instance cannot be taken to be a true belief in the past, because a person can remember an instance which he had experienced, but this memory experience is again private to that person only. To quote Ayer's views on memory experience:

> It is therefore assumed that there must be some present content which gives, as it were, its flavour to a memory experience. This present content, which is commonly thought of as a memory image, is treated as a private object, very much like a sense-datum.[25]

This follows that even if a person justified his claim that there was past on the basis of memory, it is confined to his own history of sense-experiences. For instance, the battle of Waterloo was fought in 1815, but a person who was born in 1820 cannot say anything about the Battle of Waterloo as he was not born at that time. Thus Ayer says: "To remember an event is to be disposed to state a fact about the past, but not just any fact about the past; it must be a fact which one has oneself observed. . . ."[26] Nevertheless, Ayer supposes that memory cannot be the basis on which we can justify our claim in the existence of past events. He maintains that we do not have

---

24. A.J. Ayer, *The Problem of Knowledge*, p. 134.
25. Ibid., p. 43.
26. A.J. Ayer, "Statements About the Past", in his *Philosophical Essays*, p. 71.

any guarantee that our memories are veridical. We may not be able to recall the situation properly. Proceeding further, Ayer argues:

> That whatever the content of a memory experience, it acquires its reference to the past only through being interpreted. But from this it follows that the identification of anything as a memory presupposes an understanding of what is meant by being past. And if this understanding is presupposed by memory, it cannot be founded on it.[27]

This shows that, according to Ayer, to remember something one must be aware of what he claims to remember is past, and thus one cannot be said to have remembered at all unless he has the concept of past under which he arranges the events in question. In such a situation, maintains Ayer, there is no hope of deriving past from memory. In fact, Ayer cannot talk about memory experiences, since there is no identical continuous substantial self which can restore memory experiences.

Realising that memory experiences do not connect us with the past events, Ayer tries to find an alternative through which one can derive the concept of past. He conceives that notion of temporal precedence is given in sense-experience, and that this, together with the notion of the present, will yield the concepts of both past and future. Trying to elaborate this point, Ayer says:

> To say that a person occupies, at a given moment, a definite position in time is just to say that at least one of the class of the simultaneous events which constitutes the moment in question is an event in that person's history. The fact that a certain series of events constitutes his history fixes his temporal standpoint. To ask whether he could have had a different standpoint is to ask whether a difference in temporal relations of the events, and perhaps also a consequential

27. A.J. Ayer, op. cit., pp. 150-51.

> difference in the character of his history itself, is consistent with his remaining the same person; and the answer to this depends upon what we choose to understand by being the same person? That one's temporal position continually changes is simply the fact that the events which collectively . . . stand to each other in relations of temporal succession[28]

The upshot of this lengthy quotation is that the notion of the present is definable ostensively as the class of events that is contemporaneous with a particular event that one chooses to indicate at the given moment. Accordingly, conceives Ayer, the past can be defined as the class of events earlier than the present. However, the argument that Ayer uses in ruling out the possibility that the concept of "past" can be derived from memory is also applicable to the idea of deriving the past from the notion of temporal succession in sense-experiences. Because, like memory experiences the notion of temporal succession in events is also private to one's own self. Above all, if there are certain statements about the past which an individual has not witnessed since he was not born at that time, then does it mean to say that those statements about the past are not true. Perhaps, Ayer is going too far by doubting everything.

Now the other aspect to consider is Ayer's epistemological standpoint. Let us apply his own theory of verification to the problems of other minds and statements about the past. For instance, take the statement "John is suffering from toothache." Generally, we see his swollen face, hear his groans and look into his mouth and see the decayed tooth. But, for Ayer, this is an unverifiable metaphysical nonsense, since, even in principle, it is not possible to experience John's pain.

Same is the case with the statements about the past. For instance, consider the statement "Dinosaurs existed in Mesozoic period on the earth." Again it will be an unverifiable nonsense,

28. A.J. Ayer, op. cit., pp. 182-83.

as per Ayer's conception, since we cannot have direct acquaintance with the past. By all means, it is true that we cannot experience past directly, since time is unidimensional; hence is irreversible. This does not mean that we can have no valid grounds for accepting the existence of such and such animal in the past. By seeing and touching certain objects of an appearance, we would be able to tell these are fossils of such and such an animal provided we have some background knowledge of paleontology. Here our meaning of verification is practical but not having mere sensory experience. Accordingly, we conceive that the verification of these objects is such that they belong to the class of fossils with which paleontologists agree to call fossil remains of dinosaurs of Mesozoic period. For Ayer, this might appear to be a metaphysical nonsense, because how can one believe in an event or an instance that took place million years ago outside one's own sensory experience. Thus, we cannot speak about anything outside the limits of our own sense-experiences. The whole world shrinks into the narrow compass of one's own immediate present sense-experience.

The philosophy of Ayer continues to interpret scientific truth in terms of sensory-experiences, not with the constitution of the laws of objective reality.

8

Concluding Remarks

AFTER a careful examination of A.J. Ayer's logical positivism, we have arrived at the following conclusions. The whole account of Ayer's philosophy discussed in this study shows that the thesis of logical positivism rests on two basic aspects. They are: (1) the principle of verification, a basic principle of logical positivists, which constitutes the core of logical positivist epistemology; and (2) sense-data, the ultimate constituents of the reality, which represent the ontological status of logical positivism.

Ayer considers that knowledge is obtained through sense-experience, i.e. knowledge cannot transcend the limits of sensory experience. This very conception of Ayer restricts knowledge to appearances of things or phenomena only. It can never penetrate into the essences of things. Then the question that arises is: What are the objects of knowledge that are given in sense-experience? Ayer maintains that the only objects of knowledge that are immediately given in sense-experience are only sense-data, which are discrete, unconnected, but not material or physical objects. Ayer arrives at this conclusion by introducing the "argument from illusion." Further, Ayer holds that material objects are nothing but "logical constructs" out of these sense-data. Thus, his phenomenalistic reduction of material objects into sense-data leads to the view that the existence of material objects is inferred from sense-data. For example, a chair in which numerous sense-data are grouped together and so presents the chair that is normally perceived are the basic constituents of knowledge. Therefore, the ultimate grounds of verification are "primitive atomic" elements called sense-data, which are directly given in sense-experience. In this way, Ayer arrives at his ontological position. This is the general position of the logical positivists.

Ayer's theory of causation is an outcome of his ontological position. As it is shown elsewhere, for Ayer the ultimate reality consists of sense-data. There is no continuity in them. It follows from this that there is no necessary causal connection between one event and the other in the reality excepting a kind of regularity (temporal succession) which is observable. This very notion of causation of Ayer led to the problem of induction, namely, what justification do we have to believe in the view that events which occurred in the past will also occur in future under given conditions? Ayer, like Hume, argues that there is no justification for this inductive reasoning unless one experiences it.

Further, Ayer provides a phenomenalistic analysis of "self." He argues that self is nothing but a bundle of sense-data or sense-contents. Thus, he subscribes to the view of David Hume. He opines that no two selves can share the same sense-data. For that matter, even the same self cannot share its experiences, since there is no continuity in the sense-data that are composed in the self. It shows that each person's experiences are private to his own self. No one denies this fact, since it is humanly impossible to share others' feelings, thoughts, emotions, etc. Not only that, argues Ayer, it is even impossible to know the minds of others. This very notion of Ayer led to the problem of knowledge of other minds.

If all that we know are our own sense-experiences, i.e. a situation in which each individual is immersed in a self-contained world of his own which is isolated from all possibility of communication with other individuals, then what justification do we have to say that others are also having similar kinds of feelings, pleasure, pain, etc. like me or anyone. Thus Ayer's doctrine ends in solipsism.

It is obvious that Ayer cannot solve these problems with his epistemological and ontological framework, because his (Ayer's) thesis is based on the premises that are objectively false. Proceeding from the premise that our own sense-experiences constitute the whole body of knowledge, Ayer maintains that one cannot arrive at the knowledge of existence of anything excepting sense-data. This very idea of Ayer is vulnerable to serious criticism as it distorts the picture of reality.

It is obvious that we cannot gain knowledge merely through sensations in the way Ayer discussed in his doctrines. Knowledge is the knowledge of objective reality which exists independent of human cognition. Knowledge does not stop short of sensory experiences. Mere sensations cannot be the source of knowledge of the things. Besides sense experience, reasoning, experimentation (practical activity) and hypothesis formation are also required. What is wrong with Ayer's account is that he considers each individual's sense-experiences are private to himself and treats the experience of each person, of each knowing subject as a separate atom. Accordingly, knowledge cannot be derived or inferred beyond one's own private sensations.

Contrary to Ayer's view, we assert that knowledge is not the private property of one's own mind. It is a social product and is acquired through the combination of various skills like reasoning, observation, experimentation and hypothesis formation. It is a collective activity of many people. Knowledge is inseparably built up by each individual's effort and is social and public by nature. In this way, Ayer's approach towards the acquisition of knowledge becomes inadequate and misleading when it elevates sense-data into all sufficient and supporting explanation for knowledge.

Coming to nature and content of science, instead of recognising the objectivity of scientific knowledge for the advancement of human progress and domination over Nature, Ayer's logical positivism reduces science to the level of systematisation and ordering of our own sense-experiences. Ayer denies the necessary causal relations that are inherent in Nature. Science operates with a system of concepts and categories which are the theoretical reflections of essential connections that are inherent in reality. Scientific knowledge or investigation deeply penetrates into the real essence of things; and it is not restricted to apparent features of things or phenomena as conceived by Ayer. In fact, science relies on the following aspects. They are: (1) carefully selected and accurately established fact, (2) a system of concepts and categories, and (3) theories and laws that explain the nature of reality. It shows that theory and practice cannot be separated from each other. In opposition to this, Ayer considers science as a set of rules or sense-data which serve to correlate observations and to predict various operations. In this way, Ayer's logical positivism is incompatible with the results of science, and its results are in glaring contradiction with the well-established scientific proof.

In spite of the fact that Ayer's logical positivism stands in glaring contradiction to actual scientific proof, there is no doubt that logical positivism is credited with posing a number of interesting problems that are common to philosophers as well as scientists. It is obvious that the representatives of logical positivism have contributed much to the development of logic and scientific method. It is true that this school of thought has joined issue with science in rejecting the view that speculative doctrines and dogmatism are necessary in the quest for knowledge of reality. Our main intention is to show the pitfalls in the doctrines of logical positivism. What is to be realised is that the crisis of positivism has been not only brought about by the internal contradictions but also by the inadequacy of its epistemological and ontological structures.

To sum up, Ayer's logical positivism, despite its repeated claims that it differs from the traditional empiricism, is in no way different from pluralist, relativist tradition, established by George Berkeley and David Hume. The thesis of logical positivism can be disqualified as a "scientific philosophy" because it does not take a correct stand on many issues. The teachings of logical positivism are basically incompatible with scientific theories. But the cause of human progress and the advancement of human knowledge demand the development of scientific outlook in opposition to contemporary forms of idealism. The development of philosophy, as an understanding of the reality and man's place in it, is always based on the scientific progress of mankind. But Ayer's logical positivism degrades philosophy into a specialised and abstract study of thinking and language.

Bibliography

Primary Sources

BOOKS

Ayer, A.J., *Language, Truth and Logic* (Harmondsworth: Penguin Books, 1975), 2nd edition.

———, *The Foundations of Empirical Knowledge* (London: Macmillan, St. Martin's Press, 1971).

———, *Philosophical Essays* (London: Macmillan, 1965).

———, *The Problem of Knowledge* (Harmondsworth: Penguin Books, 1977).

———, *The Concept of a Person and Other Essays* (London: Macmillan, 1973).

———, *The Origins of Pragmatism* (London: Macmillan, 1974).

———, *Metaphysics and Common Sense* (London: Macmillan, 1973).

———, *Russell and Moore: The Analytical Heritage* (London: Macmillan, 1973).

———, *Probability and Evidence* (London: Macmillan, 1973).

———, *Russell* (Glasgow: Fontanna/Collins, 1977).

———, *The Central Questions of Philosophy* (Harmondsworth: Penguin Books, 1976).

———, *Part of My Life* (London: Collins, 1977).

———, *Hume* (London: Oxford University Press, 1980).

———, *Philosophy in the Twentieth Century* (London: Unwin Paperbacks, 1984).

———, *Wittgenstein* (Chicago: Chicago University Press, 1985).

——— et al. (eds.), *The Revolution in Philosophy* (London: Macmillan, 1963).

——— (ed.), *The Humanist Outlook* (Great Britain: Pemberton, 1968).

——— and R. Winch (eds.), *British Empirical Philosophers: Locke Berkeley Hume Reid and J.S. Mill* (New York: A Clarion Book, 1968).

ARTICLES

Ayer, A.J., "Philosophy at Absolute Zero", *Encounter* (London), vol. 21, October 1955, pp. 24-33.

———, "On Particulars and Universals", *Proceedings of the Aristotelian Society* (London), N.S. vol. XXXIV, no. 34, 1934, pp. 51-62.

———, "The Genesis of Metaphysics", *Analysis* (London), vol. 1, no. 4, 1934, pp. 15-22.

———, "Demonstration of the Impossibility of Metaphysics", *Mind* (London), N.S. vol. XLIII, no. 43, 1934, pp. 335-45.

———, "Internal Relations", *Proceedings of the Aristotelian Society Supplement* (London), vol. XXXV, no. 35, 1935, pp. 63-74.

———, "The Principle of Verifiability", *Mind* (London), N.S., vol. XLV, no. 45, 1936, pp. 199-203.

———, "Does Philosophy Analyse Common Sense?", *Proceedings of the Aristotelian Society Supplement* (London), vol. XVI, no. 16, 1937, pp. 162-71.

Secondary Sources

BOOKS

Ackermann, Robert, *Theories of Knowledge: A Critical Introduction* (New York: Megra Hill, 1974).

Afanasyev, V., *Marxist Philosophy* (Moscow: Foreign Language Publishing House, n.d.).

Aiken, Henry D., *The Age of Ideology* (New York: A Mentor Book, n.d.).

Alston, W.P. and George Nakhnikian (eds.), *Readings in Twentieth Century Philosophy* (New York: Free Press of Glencoe, 1963).

Aristotle, *Metaphysics*, ed. & tr. John Warrington (London: J.M. Dent and Sons, 1956).

Aune, Bruce, *Knowledge, Mind and Nature* (California: Ridgeview Publishing Company, 1967).

Austin, J.L., *Philosophical Papers*, ed. J.O. Urmson & G.J. Warnock (London: Oxford University Press, 1970).

———, *Sense and Sensibilia* (Oxford: Clarendon Press, 1962).

Barlingay, S.S. and B. Padma Kulkarni, *A Critical Survey of Western Philosophy* (Delhi: Macmillan, 1980).

Basin, Yev Ceny, *Semantic Philosophy of Art* (Moscow: Progress Publishers, 1979).

Benn, A.W., *History of Modern Philosophy* (London: Watts & Company, n.d.).

Bennett, Jonathan, *Locke, Berkeley, Hume: Central Themes* (Oxford: Clarendon, 1977).

Bergman, Gustav, *The Metaphysics of Logical Positivism* (London: Longman, 1954).

Berkeley, George, *The Principles of Human Knowledge*, ed. G.J. Warnock (Glasgow: Collins/Fontana, 1977).

Berlin, Isaiah Sir, *The Age of Enlightenment* (New York: A Mentor Book, n.d.).

Black, Max (ed.), *Philosophical Analysis* (Ithaca: Cornell University Press, 1950).

Blauberg, V.I., V.N. Sandousky and E.C. Yudin, *Systems Theory: Philosophical and Methodological Problems* (Moscow: Progress Publishers, 1977).

Bobik, Joseph (ed.), *The Nature of Philosophical Enquiry* (London: University of Notre Dame Press, 1970).

Carnap, Rudolf, *The Unity of Science* (London: N.P, 1934).

Carr, E.H., *What is History*? (Harmondsworth: Penguin Books, 1977).

Caws, Peter, *The Philosophy of Science* (New York: D. Van Nostrand Company, 1965).

Chepikov, M.G., *The Integration of Science* (Moscow: Progress Publishers, 1978).

Chisholm, Roderick M., *Theory of Knowledge* (New Delhi: Prentice-Hall of India Pvt. Ltd., 1977).

Cohen, Morris R. and Ernest Nagel, *An Introduction to Logic and Scientific Method* (New Delhi: Allied Publishers Pvt. Ltd., 1972).

Commins, Saxe, and Robert N. Linscott (eds.), *Man and the State: The Political Philosophers* (New York: Modern Pocket Library, 1953).

——, (ed.), *Man and Spirit: The Speculative Philosophers* (New York: Modern Pocket Library, 1954).

Copleston, Frederick S.J., *A History of Philosophy* (London: Bums Oates and Waṣh Bourne Limited, 1959), vol. V.

Cornforth, Maurice, *Science and Idealism* (New York: International Publishers, 1947).

———, *Dialectical Materialism: An Introductory Course* (Calcutta: National Book Agency, 1976).

———, *In Defence of Philosophy Against Positivism and Pragmatism* (London: Lawrence & Wishart, 1950).

———, *Marxism and the Linguistic Philosophy* (London: Lawrence & Wishart, 1965).

———, *The Open Philosophy and the Open Society* (New York: International Publishers, 1976).

———, *Philosophy and Communism* (London: Lawrence & Wishart, 1980).

Engles, Frederick, *Dialectics of Nature* (Moscow: Progress Publishers, 1976).

Ewing, A.C., *The Fundamental Questions of Philosophy* (Bombay: Allied Publishers, 1967).

———, *Ethics* (London: Teach Yourself Books, 1973).

Fuller, B.A.G. and S.M. McMurrin, *A History of Philosophy* (Delhi: Oxford and IBH & Co., 1969), 3rd edn.

Gariforth, F.W., *The Scope of Philosophy* (London: Longman, 1971).

Gellener, Ernest, *Words and Things* (Harmondsworth: Penguin Books, 1968).

Goodman, Nelson, *Fact, Fiction and Forecast* (Cambridge: Harvard University Press, 1955), 2nd edn.

Hamlyn, D.W., *Sensation and Perception* (London: Routledge & Kegan Paul, 1969).

———, *The Theory of Knowledge* (London: Macmillan, 1971).

Harris, Errol, *Hypothesis and Perception* (London: George Allen and Unwin, 1970).

Hospers, John, *An Introduction to Philosophical Analysis* (New Delhi: Allied Publishers Pvt. Ltd., 1971).

Hudson, W.D., *Modern Moral Philosophy* (London: Macmillan, 1970).

Hume, David, *A Treatise of Human Nature*, ed. D.G.C. MacNabb, (Glasgow: Fontanna/Collins. 1975), Book I.

———, *A Treatise of Human Nature*, ed. Ardac Palls (Glasgow: Fontanna/Collins, 1972), Books II & III.

———, *An Enquiry Concerning Human Understanding* (Glasgow: Fontanna Collins, 1975), Appendix B.

Jangam, R.T., *Logical Positivism and Politics* (Delhi: Sterling Publishers, 1970).

Joad, C.E.M., *A Critique of Logical Positivism* (London: Victor Gollancz, 1950).

Jones, W.T., *The Twentieth Century to Wittgenstein and Sartre* (New York: Harcourt Brace Jovanovich Inc., 1975).

Jorgensen, Jorgen, *The Development of Logical Empiricism* (Chicago: The University of Chicago Press, Int. Encyl. of Unified Science, 1954).

Kant, Immanuel, *Critique of Pure Reason*, tr. Norman Kemp Smith (London: Macmillan, 1973).

Katz, Jerrold J., *Linguistic Philosophy* (London: George Allen and Unwin, 1972).

Kazimierz, Ajdukiewicz, *Problems and Theories of Philosophy*, trs. Henry Skolinowsky and Anthony Quinton (London: Cambridge University Press, 1975).

Kelle, V. and M. Kovalson, *Historical Materialism* (Moscow: Progress Publishers, 1973).

Kemp, John, *The Philosophy of Kant* (London: Oxford University Press, 1968).

Kharin, Yu A., *Fundamentals of Dialectics* (Moscow: Progress Publishers, 1981).

Korner, Stephan, *Fundamental Questions of Philosophy* (Harmondsworth: Penguin Books, 1973).

Kraft, V., *The Vienna Circle* (New York: Philosophical Library, 1953).

Lehrer, Keith, *Knowledge* (Oxford: Clarendon Press, 1978).

Lenin, V.I., *Materialism and Empirio-Criticism* (Moscow: Progress Publishers, 1973), rev. edn.

Lewis, Clarence Irving, *Mind and the World Order* (New York: Dover Publications Inc., 1956).

Lewis, H.D. (ed.), *Contemporary British Philosophy* (London: Allen & Unwin, 1956), 3rd series.

Livergood, Norman D., *Activity in Marx's Philosophy* (The Hague: Martinus Nijhoff, 1967).

Locke, John, *An Essay Concerning Human Understanding*, A.D. Woozley (ed.) (Glasgow: Collins/Fontanna Paperbacks, 1977).

Mabbott, J.D., *An Introduction to Ethics* (London: Hutchinson University Library, 1966).

Macdonald, Margaret (ed.), *Philosophy and Analysis* (Oxford: Basil Blackwell, 1954).

Mace, C.A. (ed.), *British Philosophy in the Mid-Century* (London: Allen & Unwin, 1957).

Magee, Bryan, *Modern British Philosophy* (London: Seeker and Warburg, 1971).

Magill, Frank N. (ed.), *Masterpiece of World Philosophy* (London: George Allen & Unwin, 1963).

Mandelbaum, Maurice et al. (eds.), *Philosophical Problems* (New York: Macmillan & Co., 1970), 2nd edn.

Marx, Karl; Frederick Engels and V.I. Lenin, *On Dialectical Materialism* (Moscow: Progress Publishers, 1977).

Mayer, Frederick, *A History of Modern Philosophy* (New Delhi: Eurasia Publishers, 1976).

Mikhailov, F.T., *The Riddle of the Self* (Moscow: Progress Publishers, 1980).

Moore, G.E., *Some Main Problems of Philosophy* (New York: Collier Books, 1966).

———, *Ethics* (Oxford: Oxford University Press, 1972), 2nd edn.

Morris, C.W., *Logical Positivism, Pragmatism and Scientific Empiricism* (Paris: Hermann, 1937).

Mundle, C.W.K., *A Critique of Linguistic Philosophy* (Oxford: Clarendon Press, 1970).

———, *Perception: Facts and Theories* (London: Oxford University Press, 1971).

Novack, George, *Empiricism and its Evolution* (New York: Pathfinder Press Inc., 1973).

Oizerman, Theodor, *Problems of the History of Philosophy* (Moscow: Progress Publishers, 1973).

———, *The Making of the Marxist Philosophy* (Moscow: Progress Publishers, 1981).

Olshewsky, Thomas M. (ed.), *Problems in the Philosophy of Language* (New York: Holt, Reinhart and Winston, 1969).

Omelyanovsky, M.E. (ed.), *Lenin and Modern Natural Science* (Moscow: Progress Publishers, 1978).

Parkinson, G.H.R. (ed.), *The Theory of Meaning* (Oxford: Oxford University Press, 1968).

Passamore, John, *A Hundred Years of Philosophy* (Harmondsworth: Penguin Books, 1968).

Pears, David, *Bertrand Russell and British Tradition in Philosophy* (London: Collins/Fontanna, 1972), 2nd edn.

Pitcher, George, *The Philosophy of Wittgenstein* (New Delhi: Prentice Hall, 1972).

Popper, Karl R., *The Logic of Scientific Discovery* (London: Hutchinson, 1974).

———, *Unended Quest* (Glasgow: Collins/Fontanna, 1978).

———, *Objective Knowledge* (Oxford Clarendon Press, 1979).

———, *Conjectures and Refutations: The Growth of Scientific Knowledge* (London: Routledge & Kegan Paul, 1963).

Price, H.H., *Perception* (London: Mathuen & Company, 1961), 2nd edn.

Quinton, Anthony, *The Nature of Things* (London: Routledge & Kegan Paul, 1973).

Ramsey, F.P., *Foundations: Essays in Philosophy, Logic, Mathematics and Economics* (London: Routledge & Kegan Paul, 1979).

Randall, John Herman; Jr. and Justus Buchler, *Philosophy an Introduction* (New York: Barnes & Noble Books, 1971), rev. edn.

———, Justus Buchler and Evelyn Shirk (eds.), *Readings in Philosophy* (New York: Barnes & Noble, 1974).

Roy, Virendra K. and Ramesh Sarikwal (eds.), *Marxian Sociology* (Delhi: Ajanta Publishers, 1979), vol. II.

Russell, Bertrand, *Problems of Philosophy* (London: Philosophical Library, 1912).

———, *An Inquiry into Meaning and Truth* (Harmondsworth: Penguin Books, 1973).

———, *History of Western Philosophy* (London: Unwin Paperbacks, 1979).

Ryle, Gilbert, *Dilemmas* (London: Cambridge University Press, 1954).

———, *Collected Papers* (London: Hutchinson, 1971), vol. II.

———, *The Concept of Mind* (Harmondsworth: Penguin Books, 1978).

Sahakian, W.S., *History of Philosophy* (New York: Barnes & Noble, 1968).

Schlick, Moritz, *General Theory of Knowledge*, tr. A.E. Blumberg (New York: Springer Verlagwian, 1974).

Sheptulin, A.P., *Marxist Leninist Philosophy* (Moscow: Progress Publishers, 1978).

Sidgwick, Henry, *The Methods of Ethics* (London: Macmillan and Company Ltd., 1962), VIIth edn.

Shullyan, Arthur, Paul Districhsons, David Keyt and Leonard Miller (eds.), *Introduction to Philosophy* (New Delhi: Prentice-Hall of India Pvt. Ltd., 1967).

Stalin, J.V., *Marxism and Problem of Linguistics* (Peking: Foreign Languages Press, 1976).

Stappledon, Olaf, *Philosophy and Living* (Harmondsworth: Penguin Books, 1939), vol. I.

———, *Philosophy and Living* (Harmondsworth: Penguin Books, 1939), vol. II.

Stevenson, Charles L., *Ethics and Language* (New Haven and London: Yale University Press, 1969).

Strawson, P.F., *Introduction to Logical Theory* (Delhi: B.I. Publications, 1976).

Surendranath, K. (ed.), *K. Damodaran Memorial Volume* (Trivandrum: Deepti Printers, 1977).

Swinburne, Richard (ed.), *The Justification of Induction* (London: Oxford University Press, 1974).

Thilly, Frank, *A History of Philosophy* (New York: Henry Holtandoo, 1914).

Titus, Harold H. and Maylon H. Hepp., *The Range of Philosophy* (New Delhi: East-West Press, 1974), 2nd edn.

Urmson, J.O., *The Emotive Theory of Ethics* (New York: Oxford University Press, 1969).

———, *Philosophical Analysis between the Two World Wars* (New York: Oxford University Press, 1971).

Waddington, Kevin, *Outlines of Marxist Philosophy* (London: Lawrence & Wishart Ltd., 1974).

Waismann, F., *The Principles of Linguistic Philosophy* (London: Macmillan, 1968).

Warnock, G.J., *English Philosophy Since 1900* (London: Oxford University Press, 1969), 2nd edn.

Warnock, G.J. (ed.), *The Philosophy of Perception* (London: Oxford University Press, 1977).

Warnock, Mary, *Ethics Since 1900* (Oxford: Oxford University Press, 1978), 3rd edn.

Weinberg, J.K., *An Examination of Logical Positivism* (London: Routledge & Kegan Paul, 1936).

Weitz, Morris, *Twentieth Century Philosophy: The Analytic Tradition* (London: Collier Macmillan, 1967).

Woozley, A.D., *Theory of Knowledge* (London: Hutchinson University Library, 1967).

Yonon, John W., *Metaphysical Analysis* (London: George Allen & Unwin, 1968).

ARTICLES

Adams, E.M., "The Nature of Sense-Datum Theory", *Mind* (London), N.S., vol. LXVII, no. 67, 1958, pp. 216-26.

Berlin, Sir Isaiah, "Empirical Propositions and Hypothetical Statements", *Mind* (London), N.S., vol. LIX, no. 59, 1950, pp. 289-322.

Bernal, J.D., "Dialectical Materialism and Modern Science", *Science and Society* (New York), vol. 2, 1937-38, pp. 58-66.

Black, Max, "Philosophical Analysis", *Proceedings of the Aristotelian Society* (London), N.S., vol. XXXIII, no. 33, 1932-33, pp. 237-58.

———, "Is Analysis a Useful Method in Philosophy?", *Proceedings of the Aristotelian Society Supplement* (London), vol. XIII, no. 13, 1934, pp. 53-64.

Blumberg, Alberte, "Science and Dialectics: A Preface to a Re-examination", *Science and Society* (New York), vol. XXII, 1958-59, pp. 306-29.

Brod, C.D., "Phenomenalism", *Proceedings of the Aristotelian Society* (London), vol. XV, no. 15, 1915, pp. 227-57.

Bunge, Mario, "What is Chance?", *Science and Society* (New York), vol. XV, 1951, pp. 209-31.

Church, Alonzo, "Review of the Second Edition of Language, Truth and Logic", *Journal of Symbolic Logic* (London), XIV, 1949, pp. 52-53.

Clement, Dore, "Ayer on Causal Theory of Perception", *Mind* (London), N.A., vol. LXXIII, no. 73, 1964, pp. 287-90.

Cornforth, Maurice, "Is Analysis a Useful Method in Philosophy?", *Proceedings of the Aristotelian Society Supplement* (London), N.S., vol. XXXX, no. 13, 1934, pp. 90-118.

Episten, Joseph, "Professor Ayer on Sense-Data", *Journal of Philosophy*, vol. LIII, no. 53, January-December, 1956, pp. 401-15.

Feuer, Lewis S., "The Development of Logical Empiricism", *Science and Society* (New York), vol. V, 1941, pp. 222-33.

Geymonat, Ludovico, "Neo-Positivist Methodology and Dialectical Materialism", *Science and Society* (New York), vol. XXXVII, 1973-74, pp. 178-94.

Griffiths, A. Phillips, "Ayer on Perception", *Mind* (London), N.S., vol. LXIX, no. 60, 1960, pp. 480-98.

Hempel, G., "Studies in Logical Confirmation", Marguerite H. Foster and Michael L. Martin (eds.), *Probability, Confirmation, and Simplicity* (New York: Odyssey Press, 1966).

McGill, V.I., "An Evaluation of Logical Positivism", *Science and Society* (New York), vol. I, 1936-37, pp. 45-80.

Rozenthal, M., "How Philosophical Categories Develop", *Problems of the Contemporary World* (Moscow), vol. XXX, no. 30, 1979, pp. 108-30.

Rubinstein, S.L., "Consciousness in the Light of Dialectical Materialism", *Science and Society* (New York), vol. X, 1946, pp. 252-61.

Stebing, Susan, "Ayer's Language Truth and Logic", *Mind* (London), N.S., vol. XLV, no. 45, 1936, pp. 356-60.

Wisdom, John, "Metaphysics and Verification", *Mind* (London), N.S., vol. XLVII, no. 47, 1938, pp. 451-63.

———, "Is Analysis a Useful Method in Philosophy?", *Proceedings of the Aristotelian Society Supplement* (London), N.S., vol. XIII, no. 13, 1934, pp. 65-89.

———, "Note on the New Edition of Professor Ayer's Language, Truth and Logic", *Mind* (London), N.S., vol. LVII, no. 57, 1948, pp. 403-14.

INTERVIEW

Ayer, A.J., "His Not Reason Why", *The Observer* (London), 24 February 1980.

Index